# Houseboats
## AQUATIC ARCHITECTURE OF SAUSALITO

Kathy Shaffer, AIA

# Dedication

To Brad

**Other Schiffer Books on Related Subjects**
*Greetings from San Francisco.* Mary Martin & Nathaniel Wolftang-Price.
*Windjammers of the Pacific Rim.* Jim Gibbs.

Copyright © 2007 by Kathy Shaffer
Library of Congress Control Number: 2007926611

All rights reserved. No part of this work may be reproduced or used in any form or by any means—graphic, electronic, or mechanical, including photocopying or information storage and retrieval systems—without written permission from the publisher.

The scanning, uploading and distribution of this book or any part thereof via the Internet or via any other means without the permission of the publisher is illegal and punishable by law. Please purchase only authorized editions and do not participate in or encourage the electronic piracy of copyrighted materials.

"Schiffer," "Schiffer Publishing Ltd. & Design," and the "Design of pen and ink well" are registered trademarks of Schiffer Publishing Ltd.

Cover design by Bruce Waters
Type set in Zapf Humanist Dm BT/New Baskerville BT

ISBN: 978-0-7643-2722-3
Printed in China

Note: All interviews for this book were conducted in confidentiality, and the names of interviewees are withheld, if requested, by mutual agreement.

Published by Schiffer Publishing Ltd.
4880 Lower Valley Road
Atglen, PA 19310
Phone: (610) 593-1777; Fax: (610) 593-2002
E-mail: Info@schifferbooks.com

For the largest selection of fine reference books on this and related subjects, please visit our web site at **www.schifferbooks.com**
We are always looking for people to write books on new and related subjects. If you have an idea for a book please contact us at the above address.

This book may be purchased from the publisher.
Include $3.95 for shipping.
Please try your bookstore first.
You may write for a free catalog.

In Europe, Schiffer books are distributed by
Bushwood Books
6 Marksbury Ave.
Kew Gardens
Surrey TW9 4JF England
Phone: 44 (0) 20 8392-8585; Fax: 44 (0) 20 8392-9876
E-mail: info@bushwoodbooks.co.uk
Website: www.bushwoodbooks.co.uk
Free postage in the U.K., Europe; air mail at cost.

# Contents

Acknowledgments — 4
Preface — 5
Introduction — 7
Chapter One: Sausalito and Richardson Bay: A Unique Geographic Area — 9
Chapter Two: Underwater Lots — 20
Chapter Three: The Developers — 27
Chapter Four: The Marinas and Their History — 42
Chapter Five: The Evolution of Houseboat Design and Construction — 80
Chapter Six: The Future — 196
Bibliography — 207

# Acknowledgments

It is impossible to list all the people who contributed to this book. I am indebted to all of the people who talked to me, invited me into their homes, and shared their stories, since without their kindness this book would not have been possible. A special thanks to Frances and John Anshen, Ed Beattie, Hugh Lawrence, Colleen and J. Herb Madden, Ted Rose, and especially my husband, Brad, for all of his help.

# Preface

This book looks at the relationship of architecture and culture in an unplanned community that developed in California in the late 1940s. One must look at the history alongside the architecture to make these correlations. But in the Sausalito, Waldo Point, and Richardson Bay houseboat communities, there is no one story agreed upon for an event, a person's life, and even who owned or designed a houseboat. People might argue who had title over a boat, who built it, who designed it, who lived in it, and even sometimes, who might have caused it to sink. Since most of the boats are undocumented (not registered with the State of California or Coast Guard), the only history that can be followed consists of a few books, newspaper and magazine articles, television documentaries, old photos, and personal conversations with the people who lived there.

Few people considered documenting the actual start of this community, and some who did took unfavorable photos to encourage "negative press" for the area so the government would take legal action to forcibly remove the houseboats and their residents. To convey the community's culture during its many early incarnations, these pages relate numerous stories that have a degree of truth and try to describe situations documented in fading photographs and distant memories. Other historians can attempt to describe a purely factual history, though much has changed, the people have moved on or passed away, and the details of the actual events that took place are as different as the people telling the stories.

In the course of interviewing people from the community, I learned that everyone had a story to tell. A personal experience, a story heard third or fourth hand, a memory from one of the houseboat parties—all were told with an intense conviction of truth. I found that most of the stories *were* based on fact, with a kind of "creative evolution." One resident who has lived there since the early seventies, for example, remembered a reporter telling him, "that's not very exciting…I'm going to need to embellish it…" (Tiche, pers. comm.)

The evolution of these stories is indeed fascinating. Several people told me that one of the houseboats, the *Taj Mahal*, literally had a "submarine airlock" in the basement. Talking to the builder, Forbes Kiddoo, he clarified that actually just a watertight door exists between each room in the basement. But then one wonders…is Kiddoo protecting the secret of the houseboat, now owned by one of the wealthiest men in the country? Maybe he's just not telling us. And the story continues…

Another resident described the interior of Forbes Island in elaborate detail: a "brothel" interior featuring red and gold, velvet, dim lighting, a huge bar (maybe two or three)… and an organ in every room. Though Forbes Island is unique, it certainly does not have all of these elements. However, today it has been changed into a restaurant so perhaps it *used* to be like that? And that story continues as well…

Adding to the intrigue of these stories is the underlying fact that for so many years residents were told the houseboats were "illegal"—many people think that the real truth is being hidden to protect the community's existence.

At the north end of Richardson Bay is Waldo Point Harbor, claimed to be the largest houseboat harbor in Richardson Bay and, some say, the United States.

# Introduction

When I first saw the houseboat communities along the Sausalito waterfront and the rest of the west side of Richardson Bay in the early 1990s, the area was not very approachable. People were living in trailers on floats in the bay, in floating shells of historic boats, in houses that were built with scraps of materials on concrete barges, and even in their vans—some on floats and some on land. Goats and chickens wandered through some of the parking lots, an odd sight only a few miles from San Francisco. This community was sprinkled all across the waterfront from Napa Street in Sausalito to the end of Bridgeway at the north end of town.

Over the next fifteen years, things changed quite drastically. Today, the community is a more organized one, with fewer derelict boats and larger, million dollar, box-like houseboats on floating concrete barges with basements. Later I learned that it had taken only about fifty years for the community to grow from very poor to comparably very rich.

The houseboat owners I spoke with—particularly those that were involved from the very beginning—stressed that one needed to understand the political and cultural events that were occurring during this community's birth and evolution to understand why it is what it is today. Those events, plus the people and the geographic setting, formed a community and an architectural style that probably could not be duplicated today.

This type of architectural analysis has long been of interest to me. Eighteen years ago, while obtaining an Architectural Degree at Louisiana Tech University, I proposed a theory regarding a "correlation model for analyzing prehistoric Cypriot culture." Published in 1989 in E. Peltenberg's book, *Early Society in Cyprus*, this theory suggested that a correlation method of analyzing cultural trends and built form could provide valuable insight into an unknown culture. It went on to suggest that as cultural events change, built form will change—and as built form changes, cultural change will follow as a result. (Peltenberg, 1989, p. 64)

The architectural elements of this book seek to test the theory of culture and built form being correlated with each other. In order to do this, one must first look at the geography and the key people involved with the community, then examine the events occurring parallel to the time of its most creative and unique development.

Houseboats in Richardson Bay come in all shapes and sizes. Shown here is one of the largest and oldest houseboats—a retired ferry dating from the early 1900s.

A houseboat as a sculpture, anchored in Richardson Bay off of Sausalito.

One of the smallest houseboats.

One of the most expensive houseboats in Sausalito.

Chapter 1
# Sausalito and Richardson Bay: A Unique Geographic Area

Sausalito is located on the western shore of Richardson Bay, one of the arms of San Francisco Bay. The Marin Headlands to the west and Mount Tamalpais, plus the foothills to the north, provide protection from the prevailing west to northwest winds.

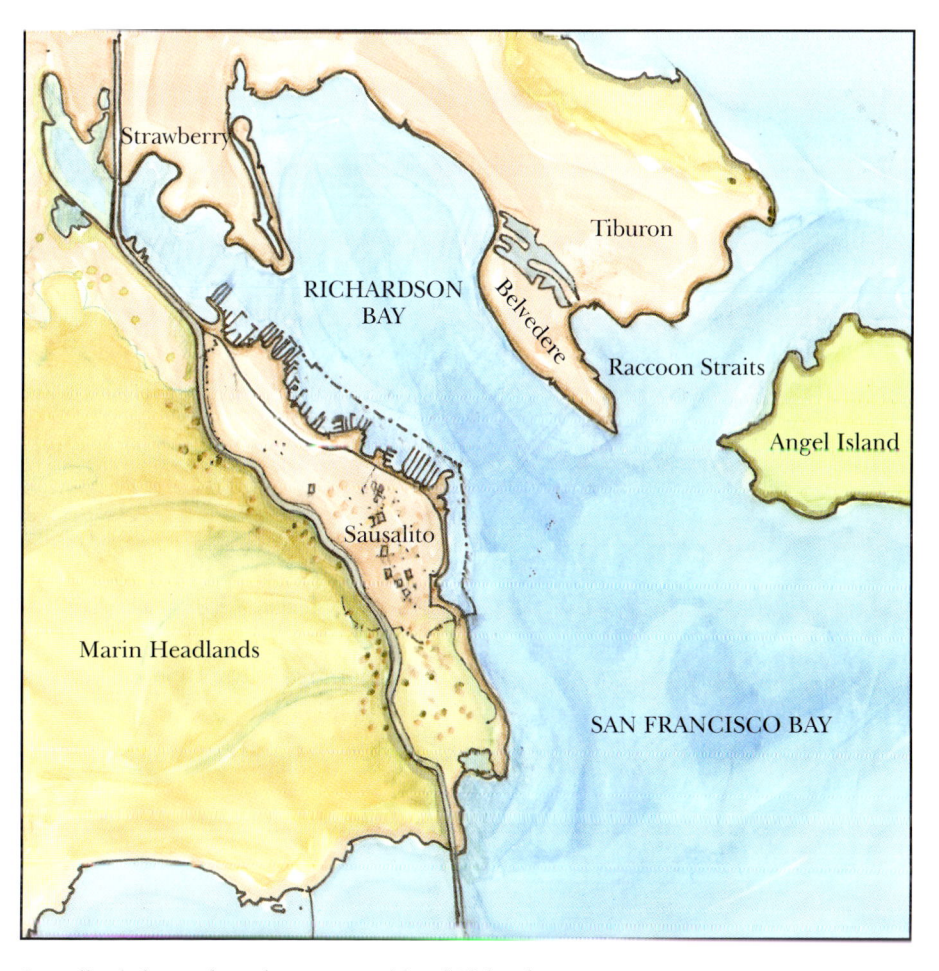

Sausalito is located on the western side of Richardson Bay.

Sausalito marinas fill the waterfront on the western side of Richardson Bay.

Looking south, down the arm of Richardson Bay toward San Francisco. Anchored boats and marinas off Sausalito are in the foreground; behind them can be seen the shipping channel in San Francisco Bay and the city beyond.

The north end of Richardson Bay is calmer in both weather and activity. Shown here, a morning at Commodore Houseboat Marina.

At the south end of the bay, cool fog frequently rushes over the hill, creating a cool climate during the hot summer. There are two tides a day, rising and falling about six feet, and a current that ranges from less than one knot to six, depending on the season and where you are in the bay.

At the north end of the bay, the temperatures are warmer, the water is shallower and brackish, and the currents are less strong.

Cool fog frequently rushes in from the Pacific Ocean over the Marin Headlands towards Sausalito and Richardson Bay.

Highway 101, which divides Sausalito from the rest of Marin County, rises up Waldo Grade behind the houseboats at Kappa's Houseboat Harbor.

There are two tides a day. At low tide, the houseboats in Sausalito Yacht Harbor are hidden behind the breakwater.

At high tide, the houseboats rise above the breakwater.

Waldo Point Harbor. The hills of Sausalito and Waldo Grade can be seen beyond. These hills typically protect the north end of the bay from prevailing winds, making it a perfect location for houseboats.

The shores of Sausalito were at one time quiet wetlands, and ships anchored in Richardson Bay in the lee of the hills as early as 1775. (Tracy, 1993, p. 2) The town developed slowly, but by the 1900s docks and shipyards lined the waterfront, a train crossed over the bay from Tiburon and ran along the waterfront to the ferry terminal, and numerous commercial transport barges and fishing boats anchored or docked along the waterfront to offload their goods.

Beyond Highway 101 are the tidelands and marshes in Mill Valley. Mount Tamalpias and the Marin headlands are seen in the distance.

At low tide, the waterfront on the Sausalito side of Richardson Bay resembles an archealogical dig of maritime history. Here, remnants of ships and barges emerge along the shore at Kappas Houseboat Harbor.

13

An old photo of Richardson Bay, probably dating to the late 1800s. A tidal marsh separated the bay from the hills. *Courtesy J.H. Madden.*

Houseboats, also known as "arks" at the time of the photo, anchored off the hills at the turn of the twentieth century. *Courtesy J.H. Madden.*

An early photo of the Sausalito waterfront. A similar photo in Jack Tracy's book, *Sausalito Moments in Time*, dates it to 1890 (p. 44). As seen, the hill is beginning to fill up with mansions. This part of the Sausalito waterfront was home to the San Francisco Yacht Club. *Courtesy J.H. Madden.*

A worn but treasured photo showing an aerial view of the working Sausalito waterfront, Richardson Bay, and beyond, probably taken soon after World War II. *Courtesy J.H. Madden*.

The town of Sausalito began very small at first, primarily in the southernmost valley. It grew slowly to the north, and today ends in a jagged line toward the north end of Richardson Bay. Early in Sausalito's history there was a north-south division between the hill and the waterfront; most natives define the line as "Water Street," or what is Bridgeway today. This line developed naturally when the upper class from San Francisco and abroad built homes on the hills, while their servants and tradesmen lived and worked "on the water or on what little flat land Sausalito had." (Tracy, 1993, p. 140) A train that ran along Water Street with a third "hot" rail. (Madden, pers. comm.) furthered the divide, and when saloons and gamblers added to the mix on the waterfront, the division became wider still. The two groups have been called a variety of names, from Hill Climbers or Hill People for the people on the west side of Bridgeway, to Water Rats or Water Squatters for those on the east side. It is much different today, with the railroad track and almost all of the shipyards gone.

Downtown Sausalito and homes on the hills in 2000.

Just over the hill lies the Marin Headlands, the ocean, and the beaches, all within twenty miles of Sausalito's waterfront. Bike trails and walking paths follow the water, connecting Sausalito to Mill Valley and the rest of Marin County. There is a wildlife sanctuary in the northern part of the bay, near what is now Strawberry Point in Richardson Bay.

Sailing in Richardson Bay, with the houses of Belvedere on the east side of Richardson Bay beyond. A visiting boat is anchored off shore. During the summer, boats often anchor off Sausalito on their way up and down the Pacific coast or around San Francisco Bay.

A view of Kappas Houseboat Marina at the north end of the bay, with Mount Tamalpias in the background.

Wildlife in Richardson Bay is diverse and abundant. The Richardson Bay Special Area Plan estimates that approximately 55 species of fish live in the bay, and a number of other fish migrate through the waters, including striped bass and steelhead trout. Bait fish like herring, anchovy, and smelt attract mammals, such as harbor seals, and birds. Even whales have been seen entering the bay.

The bay is also visited by hundreds if not thousands of migrating birds. During regular observations, the Audubon society labeled the mudflats as a shorebird refuge: "Small shorebirds, such as western and least sandpipers and dunlin, feed in the mud flats during low tide." (Letter to Robert Hickman, BCDC, 2-23-88 by Barbara Salzmann, Chair) Since much of the upland habitat has been lost to development and human uses, the birds roost on floating log rafts and pilings across the waterfront.

Wild geese at Waldo Point Harbor.

Seals sun themselves on the breakwater in Clipper Yacht Harbor, adjacent to the Waldo Point Harbor houseboat marina.

A heron rests on a piling at Commodore Marina.

Shorebirds on Richardson Bay near Commodore Marina.

Geese in Richardson Bay.

18

An egret and a heron near the end of Napa Street by Galilee Harbor, a few blocks from downtown Sausalito.

Pelicans roosting off Waldo Point, near the north end of Richardson Bay. *Courtesy of Pat Lawrence.*

# Chapter 2
# Underwater Lots

## History of the Underwater Lots

The shipyards, houseboat communities, and marinas in Sausalito would not have developed to the extent that they did had not the United States government and the California state legislature decided to sell the tidelands in San Francisco Bay (plus all of its tributaries and arms) in the mid-1800s.

As early as 1847, before Mexico transferred California to the United States, Brigadier General Stephen Kearny set the tone that the San Francisco Bay was available for reclamation and development. At this time, Kearny granted beach and water lots in Yuerba Buena Cove to the town of San Francisco; these lots could be sold to raise money for the benefit of the town. This area is now the heart of the financial district in San Francisco. (Scott, 1963, p. 1)

When California attained statehood in 1850, Congress was vague about what should be done with these tidelands, stating "…all the navigable waters within the state shall be common highways, forever free, as well as to the inhabitants of said state as to the citizens of the United States, without any tax, impost, or duty therefore." (p.1, quoting Public Laws of the U.S., 1st sess., 31st Cong., 1850, pp. 452-453) This became a controversial subject, but Governor John Bigler was able to successfully argue that the "shores of navigable waters, and the soils under them, were not granted by the Constitution to the United States, but were reserved to the states respectively; and the new states have the same rights, sovereignty, and jurisdiction over this subject as the original states." (p. 1, quoting Pollard, 1845) Thus, the precedent was set that San Francisco Bay's tidelands could be sold.

In 1868, the state legislature established the State Land Office and the Board of Tide Land Commissioners (known today as the State Board of Tide Land Commissioners) to raise money for the state though the sale of these tide land lots. Much of the land in the southern arm of San Francisco Bay was sold to industry; among the purchasers were the Morgan Oyster Company, Pacific Portland Cement Company, and the Ideal Cement Company. Along San Francisco, more lots were subdivided "to a point not beyond 24 feet water at the lowest stage of the tide." Much of this land ended up in the hands of "realty syndicates, banks, title insurance companies, investment houses, railroads, and manufacturing companies." (Scott, 1963, p.7) An exception was the water in the north end of Richardson Bay, where several dozen private individuals bought separate lots. Along Sausalito, small underwater lots were platted, with the streets reserved for the State, i.e., the County of Marin and the town of Sausalito. This act proved very important today, since these streets have to remain open "for the purposes of drainage, navigation and the wants of commerce." (p.7)

By 1878, a group of prominent Californians had organized and drafted a new constitution for submission to the voters; it was designed particularly to protect public access to the bays from a shoreline that is now privately owned and prohibiting "the sale of tidelands within two miles of any incorporated city or town."

With the opening of the Panama Canal, the State was encouraged to build ports and help cities in the San Francisco Bay area create them. This led to the state legislature writing a statute "that gave cities control over tidelands and submerged lands in the bay area for harbor development." Cities obtained grants from the State to build ports, harbors, and even airports.

This aerial photo shows the Sausalito waterfront; based on the level of completion of the Sausalito Yacht Harbor it was probably taken in the late 1950s. Bridgeway, the main road closest to the water, was originally on the shore of Richardson Bay. The underwater lots extend out to the left edge of the photo and one can see how they were starting to be filled in with buildings, piers, marinas, and land. Napa Street pier, an actual city street, extends off the bottom edge of the photo. This type of development all over San Francisco Bay spurred the organization of the Bay Conservation and Development Commission. *Courtesy of J.H. Madden.*

By 1962, tidelands all over the San Francisco Bay had been divided up among numerous property owners and tenants, and easements crisscrossed the bay. There was no plan in place to describe how the bay should be developed, and property owners and tenants were anxious to develop their properties and exercise their easement rights. Cities were planning developments and freeways using the tidelands; private owners were planning housing developments, amusement parks, and more.

As described further on page 24, Bechtel Corporation, under the direction of the federal government, had filled a large part of the tidelands off of Sausalito from Pine Point to Waldo Point to create a World War II shipyard known as "Marinship." (Tracy, 1993, p. 158) When Bechtel left and discontinued operation of the shipyard after World War II, their tideland lots (part of them now filled in) were sold by the War Assets Administration as land and tidelands to private individuals, industry, and some small time developers. Many of the people who purchased these tideland (underwater) lots in Sausalito after World War II had plans to fill the land and build hotels, apartments, restaurants, docks, boat slips, and parking lots. (Scott, 1963, p. 37) One, George Kappas, was a merchant and developer from San Francisco. The story is told that he purchased the land at the northernmost point of Richardson Bay to build a shipping port. This port would be connected to San Francisco Bay and beyond by the Marinship channel, which was presumably to be maintained by the Corps of Engineers. A wealthy Sausalito property owner, the Arques family, purchased some of the land and combined it with their other holdings along the Sausalito waterfront. Other private individuals, like Alexis Tellis, Gordon Onslow-Ford, and Frances Anshen, were simply looking for places to escape to and bought individual lots plus the beached ferries or barges on them to live in. Other lots were purchased by shipyard owners, harbor developers, and some industry, including the "Schoonmaker Company's diesel engine rebuilding repair plant." (Tracy, 1993, p.166)

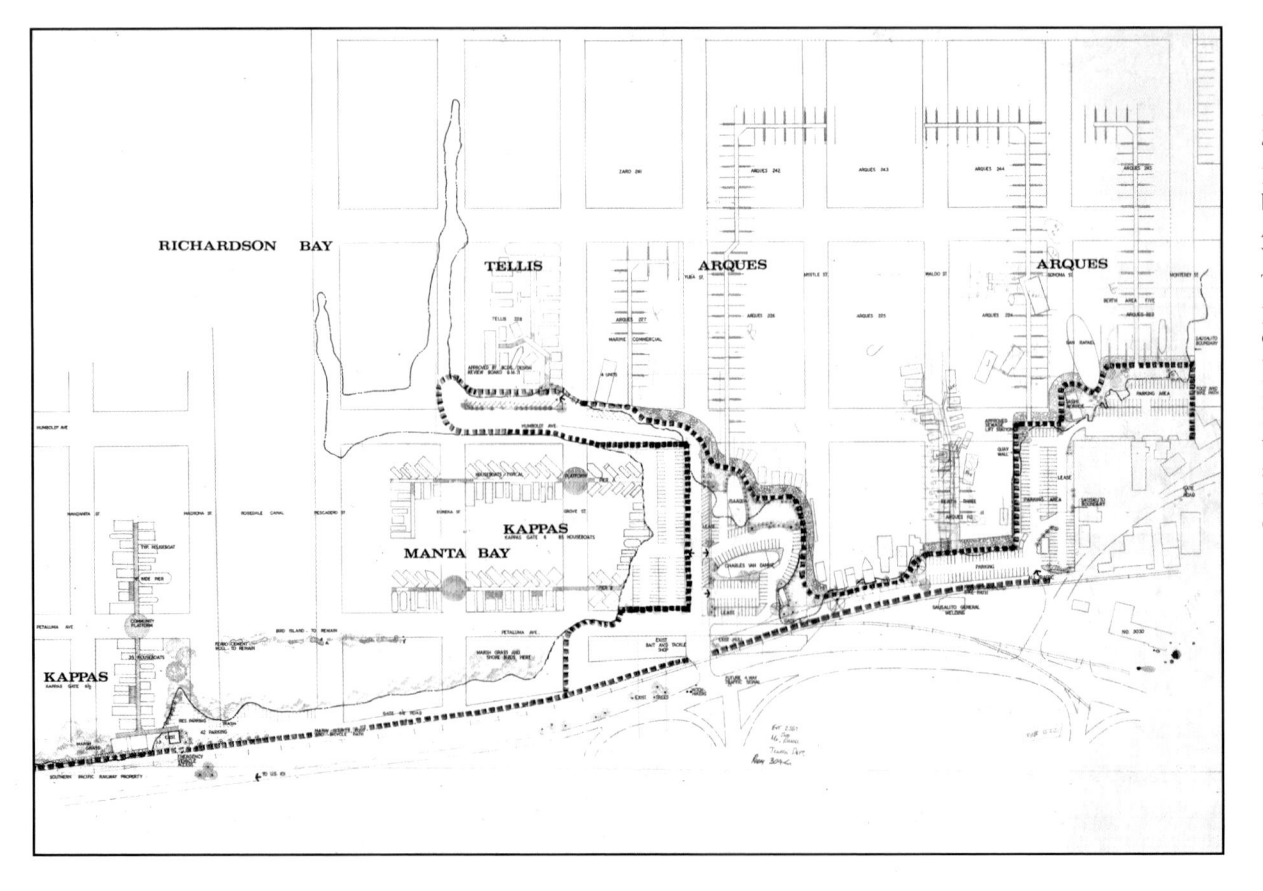

From the drawing entitled "Composite Plan for the Marin County Houseboat Community," dated August 12, 1971 by R.P. Young and J.P. Boeder. This was one of the first plans for the houseboat community and shows the property at Waldo Point at the north end of Richardson Bay. All of the underwater streets are shown, including the old names before Marinship. *Courtesy Ed Beattie.*

Concerned about the potential destruction of the entire San Francisco Bay shoreline, the Institute of Governmental Studies commissioned Mel Scott in 1963 to write a study of the development of San Francisco Bay. In this well respected report, Scott painted a disturbing picture of the bay being filled and the necessity to develop "a bay conservation and development commission." The report specifically discussed Richardson Bay ("the most beautiful of all the small arms of San Francisco Bay") and its ultimate doom. Some tideland owners on other sides of Richardson Bay had already filled in their tideland lots with housing developments, Belvedere Island had been joined to the Tiburon Peninsula, and plans for enormous developments off of Sausalito were nearing approval to be built.

Suddenly all development in San Francisco Bay, existing and proposed, was under scrutiny, and its existence depended on the approval of the new bay conservation and development commission. All plans for developing the waterfront slowed down as government regulatory agencies became involved. This precedent-setting move created the Bay Conservation Development Commission (BCDC) and either put a stop to or slowed down much of the development that was being planned in Richardson Bay—including plans for houseboat marinas in the bay.

## Use of the Waterfront and Underwater Lots

Most of the sites along Sausalito's waterfront today had roots in shipbuilding. Herb Madden Sr. was partner in the Madden and Lewis (shipbuilding) Company at the foot of Locust Street. C.H. Arques was partner in the Crichton-Arques Shipyard that began at Napa Street (Tracy, 1993, p. 137), and later the Arques Shipyard near the present location of the Sausalito Yacht Harbor. The Oakland Shipbuilding Company built a boatyard just north of Napa Street and the Nunes Brothers had a boatyard at the foot of Main Street. With Marinship located north of the Oakland Shipbuilding Company and extending nearly all the way to the north end of Richardson Bay, almost the entire west side of the bay was filled by shipyards (with some commercial marinas located within them). It was common for workers at these shipyards to live in boats or arks near the shipyard where they worked. (Madden, 2006, pers. comm.)

Only a few of the planned pleasure boat marinas and houseboat marinas were built along the Sausalito shoreline. The advent of the Bay Conservation Development Commission (BCDC) slowed—and in some cases stopped—the development of the underwater lots, preserving the wide expanse of Richardson Bay.

Early Sausalito waterfront and underwater lots were initially developed into shipyards and buildings for related businesses. This old photo shows the section of waterfront off Bridgeway where the Crichton-Arques and Madden and Lewis shipyards were located, among others. Many of the old buildings were abandoned or rented to artists in the 1950s while property owners waited for permission from government agencies to develop their property. *Courtesy of J.H. Madden.*

> **What is an "ark"?**
>
> The most common definition of an ark is a boat on piles. According to the Marin County Development Code, the term can apply to "Any Vessel, boat, craft, or structure originally designed to float that is now permanently grounded or supported by a foundation or piling." (Marin County Development Code, 22.130) An ark has also been described as a "country home of the sea-lover." (*Pacific Monthly*, August 1966)

An ark.

Of these locations in Sausalito today, only the Nunes Brothers boatyard site at the southern end of town has been replaced with houses. The rest have been redivided and replaced for the most part with pleasure boat marinas and houseboat marinas.

The type of development on the waterfront north of Napa Street can be attributed to the building of Marinship in March 1942. Before the United States entered World War II, part of this area was a tidal marsh flanked by Waldo Point on the north and Pine Point on the south. A railroad trestle crossed between the two and Bridgeway ran along the water. (Tracy, 1993 p. 156-159) A few months after the U.S. entered the war, Bechtel Corporation selected this area as the ideal location to build Liberty ships. The government condemned 202 acres, including 40 dwelling units for the site (Waterfront Residential Use Study, Earth Metrics Inc. December 1983, 2-2) and on March 28 it was leveled and the marsh was filled. Buildings, ship launching ways, and two 1000 foot long fitting docks were built (later the location of the Annicelli's Fish Pier and the Army Corps of Engineers docks). A 20 foot deep channel was dredged to connect the ways that launched the ships to San Francisco Bay. The old streets and names were removed from most of the records and the roads in the shipyard were referred to by the gate to the shipyard that the road served. This Bechtel World War II military shipyard became known as "Marinship."

Marinship went on to employ a 20,000 person labor force working 24 hours a day. (Waterfront Residential Use Study December 1983, Earth Metrics, 2-2) Fifteen Liberty ships and 78 modern turbo-electric tankers were built in three and a half years. (*Sausalito News*, 11-1-45, p. 1) When the war ended, Bechtel declared that the purpose of Marinship had been fulfilled and that they did not intend to continue operating the Marinship facilities. With Sausalito's desire to demonstrate commitment to the wartime effort, they had not asked for a post-war plan for the area. Bechtel left the disposition of the property to the Maritime Commission. As noted earlier, the land, the ways, and the buildings were then sold off piecemeal by the War Assets Administration. (Tracy 1993, p. 166)

During the post war era of the 1950s, a few private buyers decided to create an artists and writers colony on some of the smaller tideland lots adjacent to shore. These went on to become Varda Landing and Mays Harbor. One remote lot was purchased by an individual in Ohio, who then sold it to a private buyer who wanted a place for his family to live. (Tellis, pers. comm.) This was the beginning of the Yellow Ferry Houseboat Harbor.

The last of the Nunes Shipyard, one of the "best-known" (Tracy, 1983, p. 134) boatbuilders in Old Town Sausalito. For the most part, the buildings are abandoned, but this was once an active boat building facility. Photo probably from the 1940-50s. *Courtesy of J.H. Madden.*

The Valhalla, one of the old saloons on the waterfront, frames the view of where the Nunes boatyard use to be. The docks have been removed and there are no plans for developing these underwater lots.

Other buyers were told that the deepwater ship channel that had served Marinship would be maintained by the government. The Sausalito Shipbuilding Company, previously Oakland Shipbuilding (Robert Rich, President), made plans for a purse seiner anchorage contiguous to their shipbuilding yard. (*Sausalito News*, November 8, 1945) Some smaller industries, attracted by the railroad service to the area at that time, also purchased lots. A.G. Schoonmaker Company bought several parcels for their diesel engine rebuilding facility. (Tracy 1993, p. 167) George Kappas purchased land with the possible intent to create a Richardson Bay Embarcadero. Many of these purchases were made due to the belief that the Corps of Engineers would continue to maintain the deep water channel. Soon after the end of the war, however, the Corps of Engineers stopped maintaining and dredging the channel. History indicates that as the channel filled in, the new business owners were forced to change the plans they had made, and some began looking for new ways to make money off the property they had purchased.

In the late 1940s, as in many other cities around the country, the GI Bill brought veterans to San Francisco to attend schools, buy homes, and find local employment. (Dept. of Veteran Affairs, 2006) This influx created a housing shortage in the area, and by the 1960s, the shortage of affordable housing began forcing people to look for other housing alternatives. (Tracy, 1993, p. 171) Also during the 1960s, political activism at college campuses was attracting more young people from all over the country to the Bay area. (*Berkeley in the Sixties*, 1990) As these veterans, young people, and others seeking a change in lifestyle came to the Bay Area, many were looking for an attractive, isolated, affordable location, and subsequently settled in the old buildings, arks, and boats on the industrial and shipyard land and water areas of the Marinship. (Earth Mechanics, 1983) The property owners, looking for a way to make money, typically did not turn them away.

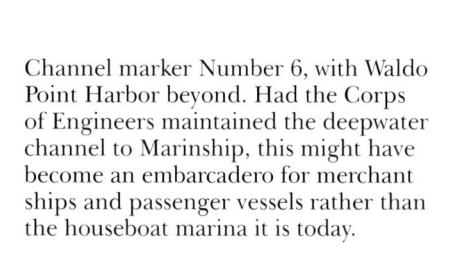

Channel marker Number 6, with Waldo Point Harbor beyond. Had the Corps of Engineers maintained the deepwater channel to Marinship, this might have become an embarcadero for merchant ships and passenger vessels rather than the houseboat marina it is today.

# Chapter 3
# The Developers

Numerous people contributed to the events that created the houseboat community, all of which collectively created the community that exists today. Among the key people were the property owners, developers, and builders, plus a local building inspection official.

## Don Arques

C.H. Arques owned and operated the Crichton-Arques Boatyard with his partner (Madden, pers. comm.), and this became one of the largest boatyards in Sausalito. The first yard was built in 1914 at the foot of Napa Street (Tracy, 1983, p. 96); another was then built at the foot of Johnson Street in 1915, near where the Sausalito Harbor is located today. As a wealthy, successful property owner and boat builder in Sausalito, Arques built many of the old piers across the waterfront, some using timbers taken from the Panama Pacific Exposition in San Francisco. (Marin Independent Journal, September 14, 1957) On his property at Waldo Point just north of Sausalito, Arques caulked and repaired boats and rebuilt barges. As was common, some of his workers lived near the yard on the shore, in arks, or in houses on poles. According to some, Arques was the first to introduce houseboats to Waldo Point. (Berdahl, week of May 30-June 5, 1972)

Sausalito looks down on the waterfront, probably the late 1940s. The train still ran along the shore. The Crichton Arques shipyard dominates the shore at the left side of the photo, and the construction of the Sausalito Yacht Harbor is underway. *Courtesy of J.H. Madden.*

The Arques shipyard in Sausalito, probably the 1950s. Many houseboaters got their barges or boats from this shipyard. *Courtesy of J.H. Madden.*

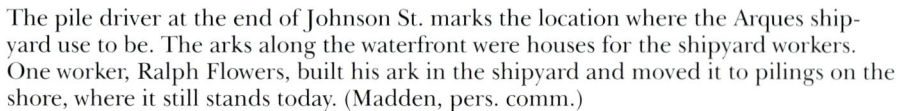

The pile driver at the end of Johnson St. marks the location where the Arques shipyard use to be. The arks along the waterfront were houses for the shipyard workers. One worker, Ralph Flowers, built his ark in the shipyard and moved it to pilings on the shore, where it still stands today. (Madden, pers. comm.)

The office of C.H. Arques' (Don's father), in Sausalito. Some say he planned to fill and develop all his underwater lots from "Johnson to the north end of town." (Madden, pers. comm.) *Courtesy J.H. Madden.*

28

With time, the Arques family acquired a vast amount of property along the Sausalito waterfront and up the Marin County coast as far north as Bolinas—as it came available. (Madden, pers. comm.) During World War II, the family's property near Pine Point and Waldo Point was taken over by eminent domain to build Marinship, but this property was returned to the Arques family when the war was over. When C.H. Arques died, his son, Donlon Arques, acquired the property. (Garlic Press, February 14, 1978)

Don Arques grew up "tagging after his shipbuilder father, watching one shipyard, then another being built." Although his background was in boatbuilding, and he is remembered for his love of boat history he went on to become more interested in the maritime salvage business. Turn-of-the-century schooners, lumber boats, hay scows, ferries and yachts would end up in his yards at Gates 3, 5 and 6 (so named during the war at Marinship). He would travel all over to pick up old ships for scrap, parts, and lumber. At one point, he owned the *Albertine*, built in 1868 and claimed to be the oldest boat on the bay at that time. (*Marin Independent Journal*, September 14, 1957)

Arques would strip out the boats' engines and other valuable equipment, hardware, and wood, and sell them to various local buyers. The stripped boats were then retired to the mud flats at Gate 5. His yard became a resource for finding capstans, ship lanterns, and other unique boat parts and memorabilia. The old steam scows were a great source of unusual, historic artifacts that designers and homeowners, many in Sausalito, would go "crazy over." (*Marin Independent Journal* September 14, 1957, p. 6)

Boat building and repair were still done in his yard, but the salvage business seemed to be more profitable to Arques, and wooden boat builders were becoming obsolete. In addition to acquiring old boats, Arques also purchased houses and buildings that were scheduled for demolition. As with the boats, he would bring them to his land and tideland at Gate 5 and anchor them there. One such building was originally the Spreckels house in Old Town Sausalito, a yacht club converted to apartments. When it was going to be razed to make way for a new apartment building, Arques bought it, transported it to his property at Gate 5, stripped out the valuable parts, converted the building from four apartments to six, and proceeded to rent it out. (Diamond, pers. comm.)

Arques also recognized the opportunity to provide young artists with an inexpensive place to live. According to some stories, he would give young people a place to live in exchange for work—offering to have them live on a boat if they would repair or strip the boat while they lived there, or letting them build their own unique houseboat in exchange for labor in his yard. The shells of boats he had stripped for their parts were a great source of flotation material for many of the early houseboats. In addition, Arques had a complete yard with equipment available to assist with houseboat construction projects. The hospitality he showed to the houseboaters who lived on arks and boats became well-known to the young artistic community, and attracted more people. Arques let them pretty much do whatever they wanted—grow food, keep chickens, goats and other livestock, hook up to his power, and use his water. Working together and with Arques' help, the community became as self-sufficient as it could, given the materials and resources of the day. Arques served as a father figure to the collection of people who came to live on his property—artists, writers, musicians, and an assortment of people, rich and poor, who had dropped out of society. (Berdahl, Part 3, 1972)

**Lefty's Pier**

The Arques property at Gate 3 was also home to "Lefty's Pier" (as it is shown on many old maps), operated by Sebastiano Sturiale, a character from the East Coast. An old hay scow was tied to the pier to serve as a landing float. During the 1950s, '60s, and '70s, Sausalito was still a town where fishing boats could tie up and unload their catch. There were places for commercial fisherman to sell fish and buy bait, ice, and fuel. One houseboat resident recalls how Lefty would barter fish and crabs for professional services.

This growing community, however, became the frustration of the "hill people" in Sausalito who had to look down on the area and drive past it. According to the majority of people interviewed, Arques had an intense, personal conflict with the City of Sausalito that could never be resolved. The County of Marin considered him "the county's greatest source of frustration along the waterfront." (Berdahl, part 2, 1972) In one newspaper article, the interviewer describes him as a "perverse and enigmatic figure to his adversaries and something of a folk hero to his houseboat family." (Berdahl, part 2, 1972) Some people attribute Arques' fighting character to his Basque heritage, others to his upbringing as the son of a hardworking immigrant.

Sausalito and Marin County became so frustrated with Don Arques and what he was allowing to happen on his property that Marin County officials threatened to close his operation. The day before the county was going to arrest him and remove the boats, he hired an attorney—over the next decade they worked to appease the county and create a legal houseboat community that would keep many of the residents he had accepted on his property. Many people thought this could not be done. (anon., pers. comm.) Arques committed to complete the project by the mid-1970s. When this did not happen, he was forced to lease the property to a real estate developer to finish the project. Ultimately, the property at Gates 5 and 6 went on to become one of the largest houseboat communities on the bay, Waldo Point Harbor.

## George Kappas

George Kappas was a San Francisco merchant who bought his property for speculation during the 1950s. According to one story, he originally planned to build an Embarcadero on Richardson Bay. Since there was a deepwater channel left over from Marinship, his property at the north end of Richardson Bay seemed like an ideal location. However, when the Corps of Engineers decided not to maintain the channel, Kappas decided to develop his property differently. (Rose, pers. comm., 2006) He took the 75 acre property and began filling it with dirt from a quarry he owned nearby. (Berdahl) At the same time, a two-lane highway adjacent to Kappas' property was changing to the four-lane Highway 101, and an enormous amount of dirt needed to be disposed of. Kappas took this dirt as well and began to fill his property, realizing that land was more valuable than underwater lots. (Berdahl, 1972) (Beattie, Rose, pers. comm.) When the regulatory agencies subsequently made it illegal to fill the Bay without permission, Kappas decided that building a houseboat marina was the next best thing. (Berdahl, Part 3, 1972)

**How Kappas Filled the Bay**

When George Kappas bought his lots, most of the property was underwater. When his plans for a Richardson Bay Embarcadero did not work out, Kappas decided that he should fill in these underwater lots—he knew the more land he had the more money he would make. In 1969, construction began on a highway near his property and continued for the next two and a half years. This construction project was producing 700,000 cubic yards of dirt a day. Kappas had his civil engineer install some stakes to mark his underwater lots, then his contractor took this dirt and started moving it onto Kappas' property in the bay with two bulldozers. (Rose, pers. comm.) When the county issued permits to build a marina and bring construction up to code, that meant filling more of the bay, and building a road as well. Building the road also involved Arques, because it went across his property, and Mimi Tellis, because she needed it to access her own marina. Working together, they all achieved their goal, although today at extreme high tides it is evident that the filled areas are sinking back to their original level.

At some high tides during winter storms, the parking lots at Kappas Marina, Waldo Point Marina, and Yellow Ferry Harbor flood, since they have sunk below the water level at extreme low tides.

Kappas went on to work with Arques to obtain the proper easements through his property to access his new marina. Since Kappas had not allowed artists to squat on the property where the marina was planned, it was laid out for ease of construction. Some liken it to a suburban housing development on the water.

Kappas' son-in-law, David Steckler, later took over the project. Ted Rose, who had never built a harbor in his life, approached him to build the marina for $500/week cash. With the help of TJ Nelson (the pile driver) and Ed Beattie (the engineer), Steckler went on to finish the houseboat marina.

Ironically, when George Kappas died, he did not leave the entire marina to the Stecklers; rather, he left a portion of it to a hospital in Greece. With time, this hospital went bankrupt and was taken over by the government. Technically, therefore, part of Kappas is owned by the Greek government. It is reported that each time the company needs a signature of the property owners (for a permit or other legal document) they have to go to the Greek consulate.

## Gordon Onslow-Ford, Alan Watts, and Jean Varda

It is unclear exactly how Sausalito got its reputation as an art center, but according to one account that is told by George Hoffman in his book *Saucelito-$au$alito*, it began in 1948 when Bern Porter opened an art and cultural center in the two identical Victorian buildings on Bridgeway. He invited "priests, mathematicians, physicists, nuns, Buddhists, along with poets, novelists, painters, sculptors, potters and weavers." The list included Enid Foster, Mary Lindheim, and Martin Metal. Writer and philosopher Alan Watts was there, as was Jean Varda, an internationally recognized artist who came to talk about color. Porter sought to get the community of Sausalito more involved in art, inviting them to gatherings, discussions, and displays, but there was little interest from the town. His center lasted three years, and he went on to become a poet and publisher and helped many great artists get their start. (Hoffman, 1976, p. 90-91)

Porter may have introduced artist Gordon Onslow-Ford to Sausalito, or perhaps their interest in moving to the area occurred simultaneously, but at about this time Onslow-Ford purchased an underwater lot at the north end of town. One story that is told is that Onslow-Ford had deserted from the British Navy during World War II and could never return to Great Britain, so he settled in California instead. (Anshen, pers. comm.)

In a 1992 PES Environmental, Inc. Preliminary Site Assessment Report, Bill Kirsh and Cliff Pederson, (at the time owners of Clipper Harbor next door) tell one story of how Onslow-Ford's property, including the ferryboat *Vallejo*, was purchased from the federal government in July 1949 by Pederson. The *Vallejo* was a decommissioned ferryboat that at one time ran between Mare Island and Vallejo, then was brought back into service during World War II to bring workers to Mare Island. When it finally went out of service, it ended up at Gate 5 (probably one of Arques' purchases) and was beached on an underwater lot in 1949, where it has been ever since.

Within a year of his purchase, Pederson sold the property and the ferryboat to Gordon Onslow-Ford. According to Pederson, in the previously mentioned report, the property was partly filled with material brought from the surrounding hills by Ghillotti Brothers Grading Company, presumably to provide access to the *Vallejo*. For several years, Onslow-Ford and Jean Varda shared the ferry, with Varda's studio on one side and Onslow-Ford's on the other. Later, when Onslow-Ford moved to Inverness, he sold his share in the ferry to Zen philosopher Allan Watts. (Anshen, pers. conv.)

A car ferry, the *Vallejo* had a main deck measuring 200 feet long by 75 feet wide. Two-thirds of this deck became Varda's main living area. He added a few partitions to create some privacy for his guests, put a kitchen in one corner, then filled the room with artwork and furniture. In this huge room, he had a constant stream of guests and frequent parties. (Hoffman, 1976) Varda became known as "a personification of the free spirit found in Sausalito's houseboat community." (Dennis, Case, 1977) Frances Anshen (see next section) remembers him as the "glue of the community." Though not a notable artist to some people, he drew people together from his connections around the world and inspired creativity. Anshen and many others believe that when Varda passed away in 1970, the driving spirit behind much of the free wheeling art community was lost and the artist enclave at the Vallejo was never the same.

The other third of the *Vallejo*'s deck was occupied by Alan Watts, who had purchased Gordon Onslow-Ford's share of the ferry. Watts, an extremely well-respected philosopher, was described as follows by George Hoffman: "Dr. Watts almost single-handedly is responsible for interpreting Eastern philosophy and religion for the western hemisphere. ...Through his writings Watts has probably helped guide more young people toward a meaningful life, and saved them from a futile existence..." (Hoffman, 56)

Like Bern Porter, Onslow-Ford, Watts, and Varda sought to make this corner of Sausalito an art and cultural center. (Dennis, Case, 1977). They created a haven for artists, and many of the people they invited to Sausalito in the 1950s and '60s stayed on and lived in their own creations—houseboats—in Richardson Bay.

The *Vallejo* today. The photo on page 43 shows a ferry of similar vintage at the ferry landing in the 1960s.

### Gate 5 and the Sausalito Art Festival

While Jean Varda was in California, he taught at one of the art schools in San Francisco, and between his students and his friends, he had the means to attract artists from all over the world. George Hoffman, in his book *Saucelito-$au$alito*, describes how Varda, along with a few others, started the first Sausalito Art Festival in 1954 (p. 178). These annual festivals became elaborate events, featuring theater, music, displays of "art in action" with potter's wheels, craftsmen, and cartoonists—even fireworks shot off a barge in the bay and boat parades bringing artists in costume to theatrical performances near downtown.

To be a participating artist in the festival, one had to be invited, and an invitation was considered an honor. This in turn brought art dealers and collectors from all over the country. It was Varda's influence that was "mainly responsible" for these events, and his connections in the art world probably helped draw people from all over the country. When Varda stopped producing the festival in the late 1950s, it was discontinued for several years, then resurrected by a few local residents. Today, one of Varda's sculptures stands near the site of today's "Sausalito Art Festival."

## Frances Anshen

Frances Anshen, whose grandmother and family traveled across Death Valley in a wagon train to settle in California in 1849, was a fourth generation Californian. Her ancestors settled in Santa Clara on the peninsula between San Francisco and San Jose. Anshen moved to Berkeley in the 1940s, then to Carmel Highlands near Monterey. Part artist, architect, and muse, in Monterey she met many artists and writers, including the author John Steinbeck and the artist Jean Varda. When the war ended and Varda had moved to Sausalito, he invited Anshen to come up for lunch one day. There, she was captivated by Varda's new home, the *Vallejo*. Varda subsequently sent her to Arques, where she bought a sinking hay barge. Several years later, Onslow-Ford sold her two acres of his property by the *Vallejo* and she moved the barge, with Don Arques' assistance, to where it currently sits near the *Vallejo*. Today this acreage is known as Mays Harbor or "Bay Haven."

Frances was married to architect Bob Anshen, and together they raised their son, John, on the boat. She slowly renovated the barge, beginning with a Franklin stove and three army cots, building from one end to the other, keeping two thirds of the boat for their home and creating an apartment in the remaining space. The Anshens were able to salvage all of the wood (mostly heart redwood) for free from a house that was being demolished to build the San Jose airport, as long as they hauled the wood away. The basic design of the hay barge remained the same—exterior walls that sloped in, hatches in the ceiling, and barn doors at each end. Reflecting the angled walls of the hay barge, two angled walls divide the living space and the original slightly bowed roof spans the 30 foot width. Lindsey Cage, a shipbuilder in Arques' yard, built a fireplace for the barge out of an old submarine net buoy.

Frances obtained the property when she and Bob divorced (anon., pers. comm.), then many years later she lived there with Wallace Mays—after whom the harbor was named for a time. During the transitional times of the 1970s, houseboaters often came and asked if they could moor on her property, and if they passed an interview, they could stay.

Anshen remembers Jean Varda as one of her best friends.

The Anshen hay barge at Gate 5 Road.

> **Gate 5**
> 
> When Frances Anshen moved to Sausalito after World War II, it was a small town. It had small houses, low rents, and simple people ("teachers and plumbers"), not the big houses, famous people, and wealth that exist today. Downtown stood two theaters, a grocery store (at Bridgeway and Princess, where the tourist shops are), a hardware store, and other miscellaneous shops. Many of the residents, from Anshen's perspective, were "arty communist types" and she compared Sausalito to Greenwich Village in its early days. One quote describes Sausalito as "more bars than churches and gas stations." When John Anshen began grade school in Sausalito, he was introduced to the class at a school meeting, and the Anshens were described as "… new, they live on the water, and the Mother is a communist." (Anshen, pers. comm.)
>
> This was the Sausalito that Anshen, Varda, Watts, and Onslow-Ford moved to, and to which they invited all of their artist and writer friends.

## Alexis and Miriam Tellis

Two of Jean Varda's artist houseguests, Alexis and Miriam (Mimi) Tellis, lived on the *Vallejo,* then the *Issaquah* (another retired ferryboat at Gate 5), until they purchased underwater lots that amounted to a little over two acres at the encouragement of Jean Varda. (Tellis, pers. comm.) They bought a decommissioned ferry, the *City of Seattle*, and, like Varda and Anshen, anchored it on their lot. Since their lots were underwater all of the time, they also brought in a barge that would connect the *City of Seattle* to the closest point of land. (Berdahl, 1971)

Later, Mimi Tellis acquired the property in a divorce settlement in the 1960s. She went on to try and create a more upscale, stable community by charging higher rents. (Berdahl, Part 3, 1971 ) Mimi was able to work with Kappas and Arques to obtain the proper easements to access her property, which is, from land, not as noticeable as the other marinas on Richardson Bay.

The focal point of the Tellis property is their ferry, now called "Yellow Ferry" because of its bright yellow color, which was put on a concrete barge basement that is visible at low tide. Rumors are that the barge added an additional 4000 square feet to the ferry, probably making it the largest houseboat in Richardson Bay.

Yellow Ferry Harbor began around a ferryboat, known today as the *City of Seattle*, that was owned and lived in by Alexis and Miriam Tellis.

A low tide view of the *City of Seattle*.

## J. Herbert Madden, Sr.

Many people contributed to the way downtown Sausalito looks today, and among them was J. Herbert Madden Sr. When Southern Pacific Railroad put their underwater lots along downtown Sausalito up for sale in the 1930s, Madden was mayor at the time. At a town meeting, he suggested that the town purchase these lots and create a municipal harbor. Sausalito was "the" yachting center in California at that time, and such a harbor would be an attraction and great source of revenue for the town. However, the large crowd at the meeting rejected the idea, thinking that Madden was only trying to further the business of his own shipyard nearby.

Madden went on to purchase all the waterfront land from Johnson to Bay Street himself and turn it into his vision—what is now the Sausalito Yacht Harbor and run by his son. When Marinship was built, Madden used material that had been dredged to create the channel to the shipyard to create the Sandspit, a breakwater for his marina. Like George Kappas, he also used dirt from the construction of Highway 101 to complete the Sandspit. (Berdahl, 1971)

One could theorize that Madden was largely responsible for keeping the open vistas along the waterfront to view the bay. The Sausalito Yacht Harbor was one of the first to have houseboats approved by the Bay Conservation Development Commission (BCDC), and these boats include some of the most elaborate and well maintained in the area.

Sausalito Yacht Harbor, c. 1960-1961. Construction of the Sausalito Yacht Harbor resumed after World War II.
*Courtesy J.H. Madden.*

Sausalito Yacht Harbor, 2006.

The boardwalk at Sausalito Yacht Harbor.

37

## Forbes Thor Kiddoo — A Builder

When Forbes Thor Kiddoo came to Arques' shipyard at Gate 3 to build houseboats in 1968, most of the speculative builders were building them on foam, thinking that the principle was to make the houseboat as light as possible. But Kiddoo, a carpenter and concrete contractor working for Local 22 in San Francisco, had a different idea and started building the first Ferro-cement concrete hulls in Sausalito.

As he tells the story, "One day I was watching a barge come down the Delta and it was pitching and rolling." He thought, "I could do better than that, so I built a barge on speculation." He credits TJ Nelson as being the first to put concrete on top of a barge, but modestly acknowledges that he was the first to begin building basements in Sausalito.

His designs allowed for an additional floor below the waterline and added buoyancy in order to build larger houseboats. Kiddoo built houseboats at Gate 3 from 1968 to 1988. His projects include a houseboat with a heliport at the end of Issaquah dock, the *Dragon Boat* (one of the tallest), and the *Taj Mahal* (one of the most opulent). He completed fifteen turn key houses, seventy-five barges, and one "floating island" (his term). (Kiddoo, pers. comm.)

Kiddoo was forced to launch the island from the ways at Gate 3 into Richardson Bay to meet BCDC permit requirements. (anon., pers. comm.) It was anchored in various locations in Richardson Bay, moved up the Sacramento River Delta for a while, then ended up in San Francisco, where it is now a restaurant. Kiddoo was also responsible for bringing a number of decommissioned lifeboats to Waldo Point and, according to some, helped to fuel a population explosion with respect to the number of houseboats in Richardson Bay.

A Sausalito Yacht Harbor houseboat, built by Forbes Kiddoo.

On some of his houseboats, Kiddoo built a two to four foot wide ledge around the top. His idea was that it would strengthen the barge and create a splashguard. The civil engineer, though, was frustrated, because Kiddoo would heat the concrete reinforcement bar to bend it into the curved shape.

The *Taj Mahal* in Sausalito Yacht Harbor. Kiddoo began the project for Prentice Cobb Hale, of Carter Hawley Hale Stores, Inc.

A Kiddoo boat on one of the properties at Varda Landing. Some residents call this houseboat "The Hotdog Stand."

The concrete barge increased the size of houseboats well beyond what could be supported by foam. This four bedroom, three bath houseboat built by Forbes Kiddoo has a helicopter pad and a covered boat dock.

A water view of the Oyama *Wildflower Barge* built by Kiddoo (see also Chapter 5). Japanese craftsmen were flown in from Japan to finish the third level.

The *Dragon Boat*. Some changes have been made since its original construction, including the installation of heavy weight materials and equipment on the top levels requiring the addition of "outriggers" not original to the design. This houseboat made Marin County impose a height limitation on all future houseboat construction.

*The Dock House* on Liberty Dock was originally Forbes Kiddoo's residence while he ran his business at Gate 3. It was originally a single story houseboat with piling to give it the appearance of a floating dock. A second story has since been added to the top. (Earhart, pers. comm.)

Today Forbes Island looks across the bay to Richardson Bay. It actually floats on a concrete basement barge; the pilings are decorative and extend just below the water surface.

## Michael Wornum – A Building Inspector

Michael Wornum was the representative for Marin County when houseboats started being regulated. Most documentation indicates that he was genuinely trying to create a balance between the bureaucrats in county government and an element in the public that wanted to see the houseboats completely eliminated.

Wornum was the intermediary between the Marin County supervisors, the public, and the houseboat community. Though constantly pressured by the public to "abate" the community, he maintained that houseboats were a "legitimate use" (Marin County's definition of code compliant building) and should be permitted to remain if they conformed with health and safety standards. (Berdahl, part2, 1972) Wornum worked with Arques' lawyer when they were trying to make the houseboats a legal use, and worked to create a building code that would continue the existence of the community and not destroy it. With his efforts, the original non-traditional architecture that technically does not comply with any building code was allowed to remain and was brought up to a safe standard.

# Chapter 4
# The Marinas and Their History

To understand the evolution of the houseboat marinas in the town of Sausalito, one needs to understand the history of the residential population along the waterfront, including on the water and the tidelands. In the late 1950s, the Sausalito waterfront was described as "a sprawling labyrinth of jutting docks, decaying shipyards and sinking piers; the homestead of teredo-eaten hulls, sleek racing yachts, sturdy fishing boats, powerful cruisers and 70 controversial homesites – 35 arks and 38 floating houseboats." (Marin IJ, July 18, 1959)

The local newspaper noted that: "three fourths of the residents are button-down, white collar types, plus carpenters, bus drivers, plumbers, salesmen, etc." These residents of the waterfront area consisted of families interested in living on the water and living independently and imaginatively. One couple, without any knowledge of construction, purchased an ammunition barge and converted it into a home. Another resident (Jerry Walters) transformed a "Landing Craft, Vehicle, Personnel" (LCVP) into a creative home with a butterfly roof. The south side of the ferry *San Rafael* was home for architect Donald Batchilder, his wife, and their three little girls, "Gina, 5, Lynn 3 ½, and Maria 2." Parents who chose to live there considered the houseboat communities and surrounding wetlands a healthy and safe place to raise children.

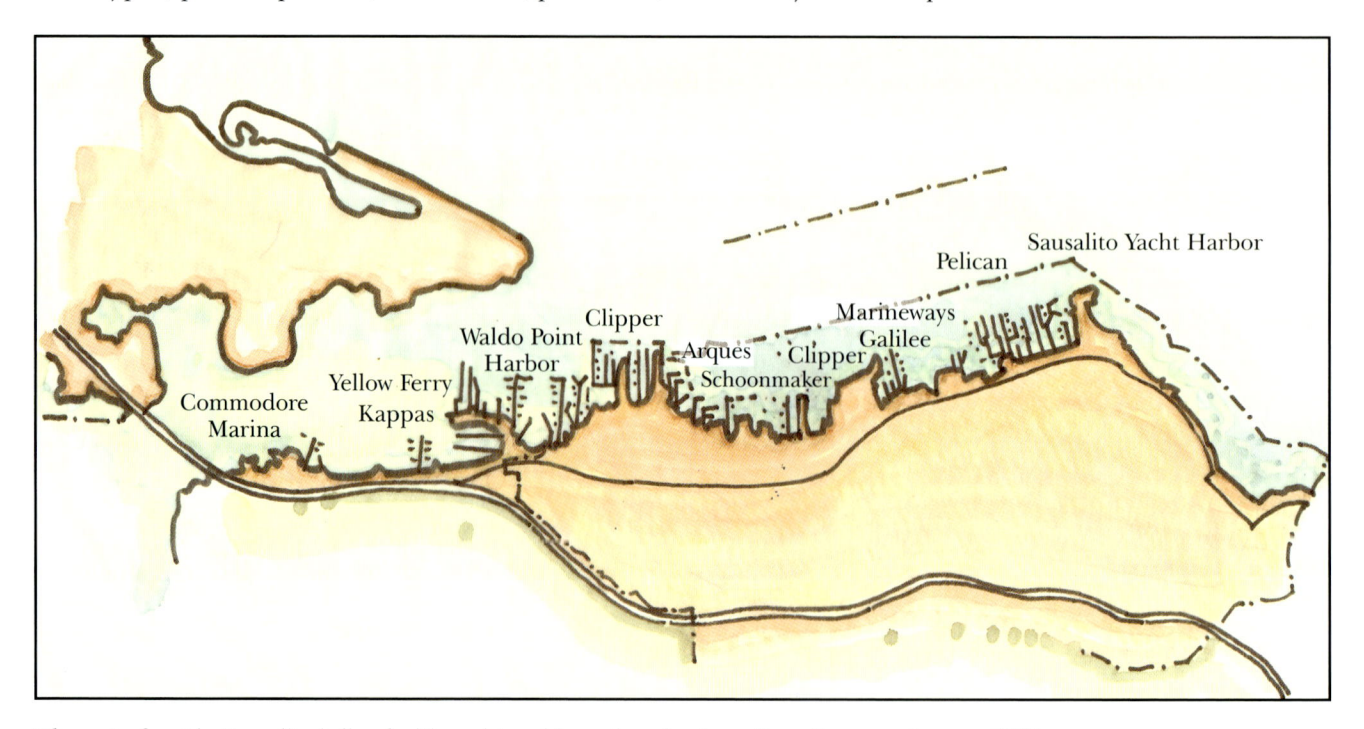

The waterfront in Sausalito is lined with yacht and houseboat harbors. Sausalito waterfront c. 1983.

An aerial view of the Sausalito waterfront, probably the late 1960s. The *Berkeley*, a ferry built in 1898 (Sausalito Historical Society, 2005), is being used as a retail emporium at the ferry landing, most of the Sausalito Yacht Harbor has been built, and beyond lies Arques' shipyard in Sausalito. *Courtesy J.H. Madden.*

The Sausalito waterfront, from Johnson Street to the Napa Street Pier to the the buildings of Marinship beyond, c. 1954. Beyond the top of the photo lies Waldo Point and the north end of Richardson Bay. Activity stopped at Marinship after the war, and many of the shipyards stopped building boats. *Courtesy J.H. Madden.*

43

### A Sausalito Sculptor

Jerry Walters, a sculptor, built what was probably on of the first homes with a butterfly roof. His idea was that the roof, in addition to being visually unique, would also cut the Bay's severe winds. His feeling on houseboats summed up the feeling of most houseboaters at that time: "You don't find creative life in a package…a home should express the people living in it." (Marin IJ, July 18, 1959)

A houseboat with a free form roof. Old photos indicate this may have been the home of Jerry Walters, a sculptor living in Sausalito in the 1950s.

In the sixties, when Marin County began cracking down on Waldo Point and Kappas Marina, to clean up the appearance of the community and stop polluting the Bay visually and environmentally some of the houseboats moved to piers and moorings at boatyards in Sausalito and the small group of houseboats and liveaboards on the Sausalito waterfront grew exponentially.

By 1980, as many as 180 dwelling units were estimated to be located in pockets east of Bridgeway along the Sausalito waterfront. They consisted of boats and houseboats anchored in Richardson Bay, tied up to the Napa Street Pier, and moored in boatyards on the Sausalito waterfront and in the Marinship. These 180 dwellings also included land-based residences, such as arks along the waterfront and boats on land that people were living in. (Earthmetrics, 1983)

Prior to the late 1970s, the waterfront in Marinship and along Sausalito had not had a lot of development, and industrial plans for the Marinship land were not feasible to developers without a railroad and shipping channel. By 1980, property owners were making plans to develop the waterfront with office buildings and marinas oriented toward pleasure boats. Houseboats were moored in many of these locations, either rent free or paying minimal rent.

The office buildings and recreational marinas were pending approval from the city of Sausalito and the houseboats and tenants were scheduled for eviction (legal eviction, since residential use of these properties was not permitted per code). In August 1980, what was known as "Bob's Boatyard" (presumably Robert Rich's Sausalito Shipyard) at Mono Street was demolished, some say by the city, some say by the property owners or perhaps a combination of both. People were evicted from the property and many buildings and boats were being destroyed. One group of residents from Bob's Boatyard, fearful of losing their moorings, organized and persuaded the Sausalito City Council to form a Waterfront Planning Committee that would sort out the possibility of legal residential use on the Sausalito Waterfront. This Committee, consisting of six hill residents and four water dwellers, was to sort out what was to become of "the waterfront area called Marinship." (p. 1) The group could not reach a concensus and ended up publishing two reports, one from the majority and one from the minority. The majority report was criticized as being "tailored to a special interest group" (i.e., the waterfront dwellers) (Buckley, 1981, p. 37). So, in 1983, the City of Sausalito hired Earth Metrics Incorporated, an environmental planning firm in Burlingame, California to do a study of residential uses along the waterfront. The primary focus of the report was "to evaluate the existing income levels and housing costs of waterfront residents and to assess means for providing long term affordable housing opportunity." (Earth Metrics Inc. 1983)

**What is a live-aboard?**
A "live-aboard" is typically a navigable vessel with sleeping, cooking, toilet, and washing facilities that can be lived in either temporarily or as a principal residence. In 2006, the Sausalito Zoning Ordinance noted that:

> Any vessel occupied in its berth for more than 180 nights in a calendar year shall be classified as a liveaboard vessel.

According to this ordinance, the specific purposes of allowing and regulating live-aboards on private vessels in recreational marinas or harbors are as follows:

> To provide affordable housing opportunities for low and moderate income households;
> To promote twenty four hour security in marinas and harbors;
> To ensure compatibility with adjacent land uses; and
> To ensure environmentally sensitive uses of water areas for residential uses.

(From 10.44.170 Live-aboards, City of Sausalito Zoning Ordinance July 15, 2003 Page 10.44-18)

BCDC allows marinas to have a maximum of 10% live-aboard vessels, and in a phone conversation in 2006, stated it could go as high as 20% for "safety." (BCDC official, pers. comm.)

The study covered the portion of the Sausalito waterfront from Locust Street to Varda Landing. It was determined that at the time there were approximately 150 residential units on the water and 30 residential units on the waterfront land "based on aerial photography and field observation." According to the study, this amounted to almost 300 people in a town with a population of around 7000. (Bay Area Census, 1980) Some units were anchored on private property or tied up in harbors, some were anchored out in Richardson Bay, and some were "land-based" residences such as arks along the waterfront and boats on land. A large percentage were tied to the Napa Street Pier. The report indicated that many of the residents did not have leased berths. Many paid little or no rent since they were either "squatting," anchored out, or tied to a public pier.

Various options were discussed as to how to address the displacement of almost 300 people if these private lands were developed. Solutions ranged from using existing housing on land to building a houseboat community in the water. Ultimately, some of the residents were dispersed among the marinas in Sausalito, some moved to the houseboat marinas at Waldo Point, and many gave up their community and moved away from the area. A few parcels of land at Varda Landing were officially Zoned "H" for Houseboat Use.

**Sausalito Zoning Ordinance**
In the City of Sausalito Zoning Ordinance, the City explains the reason for creating such a Houseboat Zoning District:

> The specific purposes of this section regulating houseboats are as follows:
> To provide a unique residential opportunity in water areas.
> To ensure compatibility with adjacent land uses;
> To ensure environmentally sensitive use of water areas for residential uses;
> To provide specific regulations governing the reconstruction, alteration, and exterior remodeling of houseboats;
> To ensure houseboat design reflects the maritime character of the area and encourages creativity and variety;
> To preserve existing water views, privacy and sunlight for adjacent homes; and
> To provide for public access to the shoreline.

(From 10.44.160 Houseboats, City of Sausalito Zoning Ordinance July 15, 2003 Page 10.44-18)

# Sausalito Yacht Harbor

Sausalito Yacht Harbor is the southernmost marina in Sausalito, with nine houseboat berths. When the shipyards closed and the workers moved on, two very different groups moved into Madden's Sausalito Yacht Harbor. Artists built their creative houseboats, and the social elite from San Francisco created their escapes from the city. Among the latter was Prentice Hale, a wealthy shopping center magnate, who began building a floating houseboat retreat on one of Kiddoo's floating concrete basements at the end of one of the docks. One of his friends built another at the end of D Dock. One of these houseboats evolved into what is known today as the *Taj Mahal*. The other recently sold and was renovated from the original owner design.

**Taj Mahal for Prentice Hale**

Forbes Kiddoo originally began construction of the *Taj Mahal* for Prentice Hale, the shopping center magnate. The barge had been built and was starting to be framed in when Hale had to abandon the project. It was bought instead by Bill Harlan, a wealthy property owner and vintner who today is part owner in Waldo Point Harbor, and he finished the project. According to Kiddoo, watertight doors were installed between each of the eight rooms in the basement; this was at the request of Hale, who thought there might be leaks. The *Taj Mahal* has an air of mystery about it, so much so that rumors of exotic details and furnishings abound; one of the most popular stories is that of submarine airlocks having been installed in the basement walls.

The Sausalito Yacht Harbor during construction in the 1960s. The marina is being dredged and the Sandspit is being filled. An old drydock gate forms the edge of the Sandspit near the piledriver. A few houseboats are sprinkled throughout the existing marina.

The *Taj Mahal* is the largest houseboat in the Sausalito Yacht Harbor. It was originally intended to be a vacation escape for Prentice Hale, the shopping center magnate.

A houseboat duplex on a barge in the Sausalito Yacht Harbor.

The Sausalito Yacht Harbor and the *Taj Mahal*.

A Sausalito Yacht Harbor houseboat built about the same time as the *Taj Mahal*.

## Pelican Yacht Harbor

Approximately 10% of Pelican Yacht Harbor boats are live-aboards, with those tenants paying a premium for their slip. The docks are connected to the city sewer and each slip has its own power, water, and sewer connection to use when necessary. Most of the boats are navigable vessels.

Pelican Harbor consists of a few underwater lots that were originally owned by J.H. Madden. In the late 1960s, Ned Martin lived in a houseboat called *The Wooden Shoe* in the Sausalito Yacht Harbor and worked in Herb Madden's shipyard. One day, he asked Madden if he could purchase a few of his underwater lots to build an all wooden boat marina. Madden thought Martin couldn't possibly afford to buy the lots, Madden needed money, so he named a high price. To Madden's surprise, Martin was able to purchase the lots and went on to build Pelican Yacht Harbor. (pers. conv. Bill Rude, 3-7-06)

---

**The Lassen**

By 1959 there were 120 houseboats "give or take a couple of arks from the Golden Gate to Waldo Point." (*Sausalito News*, March 10, 1959, p.13) In Sausalito, Sausalitans had finally had enough of the houseboat community and filed a condemnation suit against the *Lassen*, an old steam schooner tied to one of the piers on the waterfront (one rumor claimed it belonged to Don Arques), where it was positioned on an underwater street between Pelican and Sausalito Yacht Harbor. Sausalito decided to clean up the waterfront by making boat owners vacate the underwater streets. As an direct result, the *Lassen* sank where it had been moored. The hull of the *Lassen* can still be seen at low tide (see Chapter 5) and is the dividing line between Sausalito Yacht Harbor and Pelican Harbor.

---

Pelican was originally intended to be an entirely wood boat harbor.

48

## Sausalito Arks

The town of Sausalito did decide to protect some of the arks after seeing the backlash when the ones were destroyed at Bob's Boatyard. (Sweeney, pers. conv.) There are seven zoned ark sites between Johnson and Pine Street over underwater lots. As noted earlier, typically the arks were originally boats that were put on piles and used for the boatyard workers to live in. One ark was built by Ralph Flowers in the Arques Shipyard at the foot of Johnson Street, then later moved to piles where it sits today. (Madden, pers. comm.)

The arks on Humboldt (an underwater street) in 2006.

A rare, old photo of the arks along Humboldt Ave. Many of the residents worked in the adjacent shipyards. At one time, a number of these arks were built along the shore from Sausalito to the north end of Richardson Bay. The handwritten label on the back of the photo reads "507-509-511-513 Humboldt Ave. Sausalito Ca 'Fostoria' March 1969." The "Midway" was built by Ralph Flower in 1926 in Arques' shipyard. (Madden, pers. comm.) *Courtesy of J.H. Madden.*

49

The arks on Humboldt, probably in the 1970s. At this point, the arks on Humboldt were the only arks remaining on the waterfront in this part of town.

Another view of one of the Sausalito arks. The arks are just a few steps from downtown Sausalito.

The arks today.

## Sausalito Marineways Harbor

This harbor is at the end of Locust Street, where the Madden & Lewis Shipyard was during the war. Over the years, it has been called by many names, including Sausalito Marine Center and Sausalito Ship and Yacht. The property owners have made many attempts to develop the property, with little success. Little attention is paid to it by Sausalito residents and pickleweed and other native wetland plants have taken over much of the filled land. Due to the positioning of fences and buildings, this harbor is isolated and more remote than other harbors from downtown Sausalito. This could explain why many of the live-aboard boats here carry some of the unique characteristics of the original houseboats at Waldo Point Harbor during the 1950s.

Remnants of the old marine ways left over from earlier shipyards.

Sausalito Marineways at 100 Locust Street in Sausalito.

### The Mt. Eden

Sausalito Marineways Harbor was home to the *Mt. Eden*, a live-aboard yacht propelled by a stern wheeler. It is a Sausalito-built replica of an old riverboat. In 1966, the 52 foot boat was being used as a houseboat and office. Wood salvaged from the Treasure Island barracks was used to decorate the interior. "There is a sleeping area in the bow, and another area on the second deck just behind the pilot house that can be used for seating or sleeping." (Moses, 1996)

Bicycles are the main form of transportation for many of people who live in the marinas.

A houseboat, with the hills of Sausalito behind.

A houseboat in Sausalito Marineways harbor. Many residents decorate their boats with plants.

A houseboat in the Sausalito Marineways Harbor on a calm day.

## Galilee Harbor
### (a.k.a. Napa Street Cooperative)

In the early 1970s, near the location of Dunphy Park today, Ed Halperin and Stanley Herzstein, owners of the Napa Street Pier, were struggling with the city of Sausalito to get a building permit to repair the pier and develop it into a more profitable piece of property. During this lengthy permit process, Herzstein let houseboaters tie up to his pier as a "temporary income producing activity until the pier is repaired and converted back to its original boat repair function." (Berdahl, Marinscope, April 25-May 2, 1972) Hertzstein claimed the houseboats came to his adjacent shipyard for repairs and stayed. Boats tied up to the pier and it was impossible to get them to leave, particularly if the boat sank or became disabled.

Most of the harbor developers along the Sausalito waterfront—like Cliff Peterson of Clipper Yacht Harbor and Herb Madden of Sausalito Yacht Harbor—did not want to create houseboat communities; they were more interested in building pleasure boat harbors and having only a few houseboats (2%). In the meantime, Sausalito was starting to sympathize with the houseboaters, and when Halperin and Herzstein tried to evict the houseboats without the support of the city they were unsuccessful. Suddenly they were in the middle between the houseboats and the city, and unable to create a solution because Sausalito did not have an ordinance that regulated houseboats. More houseboaters congregated in the area of Halperin and Herzstein's property, later known as "Terra Landing." (Earth Metrics, 1983) As they found themselves torn between selling the pier and shipyard or trying to develop it themselves into a marine-oriented retail wharf, a series of events followed whereby the pier was destroyed because of safety issues and the town became even more sympathetic with the houseboaters than the property owners. Subsequently, a group of houseboaters formed a cooperative, or "community association," and through government funding and grants were able to collectively buy the property and create their own houseboat community.

The Galilee Harbor office keeps a low profile. Many Sausalito residents rarely visit the harbor, even though it is only a few blocks from City Hall.

Each tenant decorates his or her own mailbox.

Galilee Harbor, with Schoonmaker Marina beyond.

At the site of the Napa Street Pier, a weathered sign from the 1970s marks the site as "Napa St. Pier / A planned Residential Community / A Project of the Calif. State Dept. of Housing." Many of the boats owned by tenants of Galilee Harbor were tied to the Napa Street Pier before it was demolished.

Today, the Napa Street Pier is gone, Cass' Marina has been developed to the south, Dunphy Park has been developed inland, and the live-aboard community known as Galilee Harbor has developed to the north. The marina consists primarily of live-aboards and a few houseboats. Membership in the 38 boat group is by invitation only, and all of the facilities are used in common by members of what is now officially called the Galilee Harbor Community Association (GHCA). (Earth Metrics, 1983)

Galilee Harbor as seen from the water, with the hills of Sausalito behind.

Galilee Harbor, the beach, and remnants of piles from an old boatyard beyond. One hill resident remembers playing on the beach as a child before the boatyards took over most of the waterfront.

Dunphy Park, originally an unfilled wetlands, is now a public park. Sausalito Cruising Clubhouse on a floating concrete barge is beyond.

Cass' Marina, as described in Derek van Loan's book, *Sausalito Waterfront Stories,* was a wetlands that was dredged out before the town of Sausalito could stop the owner. Today it is a popular boat rental facility.

With time, Galilee Harbor officially became a legal marina in Sausalito through a long series of local resolutions. But, the resolutions are complex and extremely difficult for a small town like Sausalito to monitor. Many Sausalito hill people believe they do not comply with the spirit of the original presentation to the city. On a larger government level, Galilee exists based on a settlement agreement with BCDC, since it does not meet the requirements of the Public Trust (see page 69). In 2004, many boats were connected to sewers and bathrooms were completed.

The site around the Napa Street Pier had many anchor-outs, according to old photos taken during the 1970s. Galilee Harbor still welcomes anchor-outs to tie their dinghys to the Galilee dinghy dock.

Galilee Harbor's pump out station. Each harbor must have facilities to pump waste from a boat's holding tanks.

## The Marinship Marinas

A number of marinas are located off of the old Marinship property. Schoonmaker Marina was originally the site of a diesel engine rebuilding facility; the sand on its sand beach was brought in for use during castings for engine parts. (Rose, pers. comm.) Today, the beach provides access to the shore for some of the anchor-outs, and is used extensively by local kayak enthusiasts and swimmers.

The houseboats of Clipper Marina. "There's something about a houseboat when it's not around other houseboats that makes it look more exotic…," commented one Sausalito resident. Clipper has two "floating homes." (Bay Area Real Estate Information Services, Inc., 2006)

Clipper is one of the largest marinas along the Sausalito waterfront. It is marine oriented, with Sausalito's marine gas dock, Anderson's Boatyard, and numerous other small ship building and fishing related businesses. Up until recently, it also had one of Sausalito's last fish markets, "Caruso's."

## Arques Marina

Gate 3 was the site of Arques' Shipyard, the fish dock, and Jerry's Marina. Today it is simply known as Arques Marina. At one time this site consisted of over twenty acres of land and tideland. Post World War II, this is where many of the houseboats were built, hauled out, or repaired. One study documents that during the site's busiest time, it contained almost fifty residences (Earth Metrics Inc. 1983), floating and land-based, though some claim there were many more. Families lived there with their children in the abandoned spaces under the old marine ways (Tracy, 1993) and in houses that were in the process of becoming houseboats.

Builders, including Forbes Kiddoo and Tod Roso, built their barges and houseboats in Arques' Shipyard and launched them on the shipyard's marine ways. Today, Ian Moody is the only concrete barge and basement builder on the Arques Marina property and his facility still uses one of the old marine ways.

The houseboats in Arques Marina.

## Varda Landing

Varda Landing contains approximately five acres (Earth Metrics, 1983) and consists of three or four individually-owned, primarily tideland/underwater lots. The Sausalito City limits, an imaginary line not defined by any geographic feature, is just on the other side of this property. It is the only area in Sausalito that is legally zoned for houseboat use. Some attribute this to the influence of its most popular resident, Jean Varda.

One of the original buildings from the Arques' Shipyards, with some of the houseboats behind.

A rustic houseboat at Arques Marina.

Until a few years ago, the small sign tacked on the telephone pole was the only sign providing directions to Varda Landing Road.

Exotic plants on the land side of the properties at Varda Landing. The smoke stack of the ferryboat *Vallejo* can be seen in the background.

One of the lots, Bay Haven, or May's Harbor, is owned by Frances Anshen and has approximately twelve residences. The configuration of the shoreline makes many of them "land-based." (Waterfront Residential Use Study, Earth Metrics Inc. December 1983, p. 5-5) The primary residence is a hay barge. The top portion of the barge was moved to pilings and the bottom, which was left in the mud, can still be seen at low tide today.

A plan of the *Vallejo* and Mays Harbor, aka Bay Haven, in 1968. Anshen began letting people anchor on her property during the seventies and eventually it evolved into a houseboat marina. K. Shaffer 2006

The pathway to Mays Harbor is lined with exotic plants, sculptures, and landscaping.

The houseboats of Mays Harbor at Varda Landing

62

The houseboats at Mays Harbor are accessed by gangways that lead directly to land.

There are no piers at Mays Harbor. The houseboats are tied in place to cleats on shore.

The ferryboat *Vallejo* also occupies a lot at Varda Landing. This was the residence of Jean Varda (after whom the marina was named), Alan Watts, and Gordon Onslow Ford at various times in the past. Until Varda's death in 1971, the *Vallejo* was a center of activity for many of the artists and writers who visited Sausalito. Much has been written on the lives of the internationally known individuals who lived or visited there. In addition to Varda, Watts, and Onslow-Ford, artists, writers, and just plain interesting people came to visit Varda from all over the world. (Anshen, pers. comm.)

## Waldo Point Harbor Sausalito, Marin County

Waldo Point Harbor, just over the Sausalito city limits line, turned out to be one of the largest houseboat developments on Richardson Bay. When Sausalito grew north, it annexed most of the land between Highway 101 and Richardson Bay, but never annexed this small area; the reason, according to a past mayor of Sausalito, was that "there was no tax revenue." While that may have been the case when the area was a shipyard and early houseboat community, today things might be very different, given the large number of million dollar houseboats. However, by address, geography, and many local residents and visitors, this area is mistaken as part of Sausalito. Magazine and newspaper articles on Sausalito have even used photos of the houseboats at Waldo Point to represent the town of Sausalito.

The *Vallejo* ferry was home to Jean Varda, Alan Watts, and Gordon Onslow-Ford during the 1960s.

Waldo Point Harbor, Yellow Ferry Houseboat Harbor, Kappas Houseboat Harbor, and Kappas Yacht Harbor in 2006. K. Shaffer 2006.

An aerial view of the Waldo Point houseboat property at Arques old shipyard at Gates 5 and 6. At one time, this was a random assortment of retired ships, barges, boats, and people living on them. The sailboats in Kappas Yacht Harbor (aka Richardson Bay Marina) are in the deep water off the harbor and Strawberry penninsula is beyond.

In old photos, arks lined the shore at the Arques shipyard at Gates 5 and 6. Much like the ones near downtown Sausalito, they were presumably for the shipyard workers to live in. A few still stand today.

Old photos show arks and boats along Waldo Point at the turn of the century. Some historians propose that these arks were, as in Sausalito, houses or boats built in the shipyard that were put on piles for the workers in the Crichton-Arques shipyard. (Garlic Press 2-14-78) The shipyard had a single working pier (Main Dock) complete with arks and shipyard buildings. The shipyard was taken over during the war via eminent domain for Marinship, and presumably this ark housing was used by Marinship workers. It took on the names Gate 5 and Gate 6 due to the proximity of the Marinship gates. After the war, it returned to the Arques family and Donlon Arques purchased the land from his father's estate. (Waldo Point Garlic Press, Vol. 4 No. 1 2-14-78, p.1)

A reasonable estimate for when the houseboat community began would be right after the war and in the early 1950s, when Don Arques controlled the property. As noted earlier, the community grew out of his shipyard and shipbuilding industry, which allowed for a diverse workforce made up of artists, writers, musicians, philosophers, engineers, architects, lawyers, and more, all looking for a an affordable and alternative lifestyle. Families raised their children there. Historical accounts indicate that the community had its own service industry. There was a general store, Lindsey Cage's flea market nearby (to buy just about anything), a bait shop, a fish dock, and livestock such as chicken, goats, and (some say) pigs. Among the residents were people on government support, the very famous looking for a place to escape from public scrutiny, some wealthy eccentrics, and some who were born rich, waiting for their inheritance. (Rose, pers. comm.)

Remnants of old ships and barges that were worked on in the Arques shipyard are visible at low tide. During extreme low tide, old-timers can point out specific vessels and tell stories of what they were and when they sank. Photos of this area during its early days are rare, as to many it was considered an eyesore.

During the 1960s and 1970s, it was not unusual for people to pass a boat on to a friend, gift it to someone, or use it as a form of payment. "One day I was down there and near tug boat No. 4 was tied a 61 x 20 foot navy work barge...he said 'hey I can't pay you but here this is for you.' And that is how I started building my houseboat." (anon.) This houseboat, on a similar sized barge, shows the size of the gift. It has since been transferred to a concrete barge.

The population of the San Francisco Bay Area exploded in the 1960s and 1970s when Berkeley and San Francisco became the center of activity for young people wanting to have an effect on the development of their country. A group of Berkeley students successfully protested, c. 1960, against the House Un-American Activities Committee, and this was followed by student involvement in the freedom of speech movement, civil rights movement, and Vietnam War protests.

As student enrollment at Berkeley, San Francisco State, and other colleges and universities in the Bay area expanded significantly, (*Berkeley in the Sixties*), some of the young people looking to create their own unique lifestyle came to the houseboat community along Richardson Bay. Then, the Summer of Love in 1967 brought tens of thousands of young people to San Francisco from all over the country. The appearance of the property at Waldo Point, which was not laid out like a traditional marina, became so disturbing to residents outside the community that in 1968, they complained to the Marin County Board of Supervisors and encouraged them to abate the community. The complaints spurred Marin County to try a variety of ways to clean up the area, including ordering bulldozers and tugboats to haul away vans and houseboats on land and the houseboats over underwater streets (Hoffman, 1983, p. 224). But all of their actions were met with a stronger opposition from the houseboat community.

**The Marin Conservation League**

At one time, the whole direction of the development of Marin County was set by the Marin Conservation League. As the story goes, this group wanted to turn Arques' property into a park and completely eliminate the houseboaters from Marin County. One of Arques' advisors remembers that things changed when, after months of arguments at the Marin County Board of Supervisors meetings, one of the supervisors, John McGuiness, stood up and said "I don't care if they live there and I don't care what they live in as long as it's safe and it doesn't dump sewage in the bay." This was the breakthrough that gave Arques a direction to work toward. The Arques team immediately began working on the first houseboat code that addressed safety and sanitation, parts of which are still in effect today. (anon., pers. comm.)

The community at the Arques shipyard became an assortment of homemade houses.

Originally, Marin County's policy was to get rid of all of the houseboats at Waldo Point but, after that proved difficult, the county, in an effort to control the location, number, and construction of houseboats, began to prepare a comprehensive houseboat ordinance. By the end of 1968 Marin County had added to their code a section entitled "Regulation of the Construction and Maintenance of Floating Homes." Houseboat owners had thirty days from when the ordinance passed in which to apply for an occupancy permit, have their boat inspected, and make repairs. A fulltime marine inspector was hired to enforce these new laws. If boat owners did not have an occupancy permit by October 1, 1969, they were cited for violation of the code and threatened with legal action. By the end of the 1970s, Marin County threatened to have the Sheriff's department remove and destroy the houseboat if it did not comply, regardless of whether someone was living on it. It was officially illegal to live in a houseboat or ark that did not comply with Marin County Code.

### Western Planning and Research

When BCDC came into existence in the late 1960s, the Marin County Board of Supervisors told Arques and his attorney that it would be impossible to legalize the houseboat community, since its existence was a violation of Public Trust. Arques' attorney began to address BCDC by forming Western Planning and Research, a planning group headed by Fred Barber, planning director for Placer County at that time. A drawing was done by one of the residents of the houseboat community and this drawing, "the Richardson Bay Houseboat Composite," was to be used to obtain the permits to build all of the houseboat marinas at Waldo Point. A portion of this plan at the extreme south end of Waldo Point Harbor (a small part of the South Forty) was approved, and this opened the door for BCDC approval for the entire marina. (anon., pers. comm.)

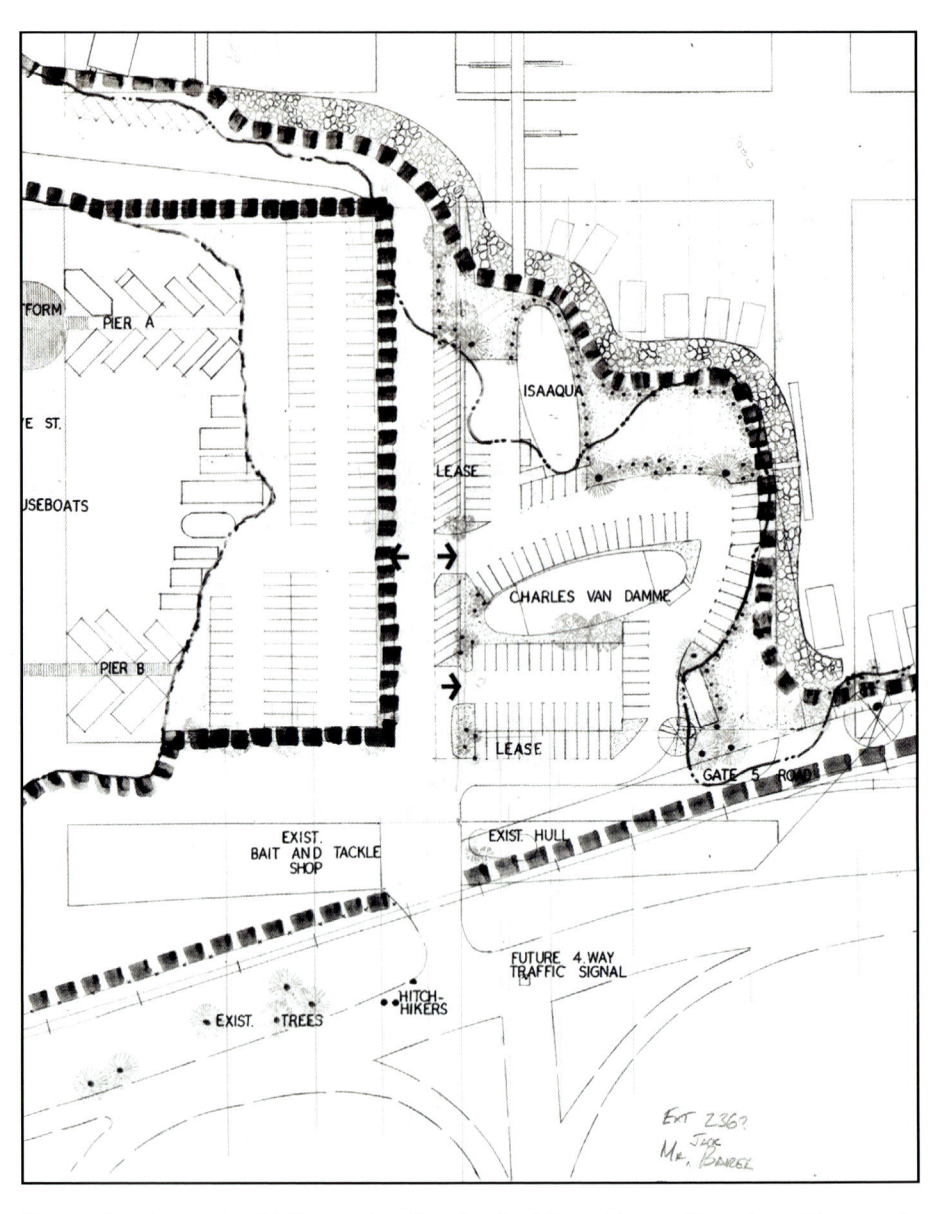

From a drawing entitled "Composite Plan for the Marin County Houseboat Community," dated August 12, 1971 by R.P. Young and J.P. Boeder. Shown here is the center of the community where two of the decommissioned ferrys are beached as a town center. The Bait and Tackle Shop went on to become a shopping center. *Courtesy of Edward Beattie.*

**What is the Public Trust?**

Early in the development of English law, perhaps before the Magna Carta, common law recognized that rivers, ports, sea, shores of the sea, and rights to fish in and use those areas belonged to the public. This concept found its way into American law, and into the law of California. (The Public Trust Doctrine by Michael Wilmar, November 1999 Spur Newsletter) The Public Trust doctrine, or easement, also had an impact on the "approvability" of houseboats and live-aboard boats on the Bay. The Public Trust easement is described by BCDC as:

> "...a property interest held by the State on behalf of all present and future generations. It applies to unfilled and filled tidelands and submerged lands whether they are held in public ownership or by private parties..." (Staff Report, Houseboats and Live-aboard Boats, July 1985, p. 22)

This means that other governmental agencies have responsibilities to assure that any action affecting these lands is consistent with the public trust. This brings in more state government organizations to voice their opinion on the development of the bay including, in part, local governments, the department of Fish and Game, the State Lands Commission, and the State Water Resources Control Board. Under the intent of the public trust, private residential uses of public trust lands is not permissible and allowing such a private use would be considered a "gift of public property" (p. 24) and be illegal under the California constitution. This suggests that houseboats would not be allowed in the bay according to the public trust. BCDC decided that when evaluating projects, particularly houseboat projects, they must determine if the use interferes with the current use of the public trust and re-evaluate the project every five years (p. 26). (A longer reevaluation period exists today.) Hence, the houseboat communities are BCDC approved, but exist tenuously, only to be re-evaluated again when the owners start to feel comfortable that everything is okay.

Public shore along the Sausalito waterfront.

Federal agencies, including the US Army Corps of Engineers, the Environmental Protection Agency, and the U.S. Coast Guard, were also were given the opportunity to have a say in the development of Waldo Point. As more agencies kept getting jurisdiction for the process, the process for legalizing the houseboat harbor became more and more drawn out.

In order to obtain permission to do any construction work on the bay, such as building a houseboat marina, government agencies had to insure that the applicant was in compliance with the laws and regulations in place. In addition to the Public Trust Doctrine, numerous laws were passed in the 1960s and '70s that required enforcement by these government agencies. Some of these laws are:

National Environmental Policy Act of 1969 (NEPA)
California Environmental Quality Act of 1970 (CEQA)
Endangered Species Act of 1973 (ESA)
Magnuson-Stevens Fisheries Conservation and Management Act (designates specific water bodies as Essential Fish Habitat (EFH)[1]
Clean Water Act of 1972 (CWA)
Coastal Zone Management Act of 1972 (CZMA)
National Historic Preservation Act of 1966 (NHPA)
The McAteer-Petris Act and Bay Plan
San Francisco Bay Plan

[1] US Army Corps of Engineers, San Francisco District Public Notice Number 20790N, December 24, 2004

Later, to add what some considered overregulation, the Richardson Bay Special Area Plan was adopted in 1984. In preparing this plan, representatives from the towns surrounding Richardson Bay (including Sausalito, Tiburon, Belvedere, and Mill Valley) evaluated the condition of the bay and made recommendations to the individual governments about zoning ordinances and codes that could be revised to provide further regulation and help preserve the bay. In their plan, they made further recommendations to BCDC. In 1985, BCDC issued a staff report on Houseboats and Live-Aboard Boats, and by the end of the 1980s, law enforcement officials began hauling out illegal boats from Waldo Point and the rest of Richardson Bay and destroying them.

**Houseboat Abatement at Gate 3**

One story that is told concerns the abatement of the houseboats on Arques' property inside the Sausalito city limits. In 1977, while BCDC was trying to control the misuse of the San Francisco Bay waterfront and ensure compliance with the public trust, they tried to move as many houseboat residents out of Sausalito as they could, believing that Sausalito was sympathizing with the houseboaters and disregarding the intent of the Public Trust Doctrine. (BCDC legal photo, August 1977) It is reported that the original BCDC permit for Waldo Point Harbor required that Arques (who owned the majority of undeveloped property in Sausalito at Gate 3, in addition to the most of the houseboats there) move twenty-six boats from his property in Sausalito to his property in Marin County, where BCDC had a better chance of regulating the houseboats. In addition, as the story is told, BCDC used this as a way to get Sausalito less interested in harboring displaced houseboat residents. (Anon., pers. comm., 2006)

BCDC had little control over other houseboat enclaves in Sausalito: Wallace Mays (Frances Anshen's husband) was tough to "tangle with," the *Vallejo* "had an uninterruptible aura of Jean Varda down there," and there was a lot of sympathy for the Coop (Galilee Harbor), particularly since one member was elected Marin County Supervisor and sat on BCDC. (Anon., pers. comm., 2006) When it came time to request an additional twenty-six houseboat berths be added to Waldo Point Harbor's construction permit, Marin County ignored Arques and his representatives and the additional berths were never obtained. The evicted houseboats either settled illegally at Gates Coop between Issaquah and Main Dock or went to the sympathetic shores of Sausalito (anon., pers. comm.)

This same story is also told (with conviction and intensity) from the perspective that Arques was "evicting" people in order to develop his property, not because of a legal requirement. This story follows the general thread of the popular line of the time—an evil property owner evicting the poor starving artist. It could be that there is some truth in both stories.

One of the most sympathetic descriptions of the houseboat communities by a government agency is found in the BCDC staff report of July 1985. Some attribute this change to the fact that one of the Marin County Supervisors, and representative to BCDC, was among the residents evicted from Gate 3. The BCDC report points out two main benefits of houseboats and live-aboards: "a housing supply and sense of social community, and within a marina a sense of security."

During the abatement of houseboats at Gate 6 (aka Gates Coop) Waldo Point Harbor, specific houseboats were called out for destruction. (Koestel, 1995) *Courtesy of Ted Rose.*

GATE SIX. 1985.

A 1984 photo of Waldo Point Harbor. *Credited to W.N. Johnson, Courtesy of Ted Rose.*

1/3/84. PHOTO BY W.N. JOHNSON MARIN CO. BUILDING DEPT.

By 1971, Arques had secured his permit from the county and the conditional permit from BCDC (no. 5-71), a 20-year permit that accommodated 245 houseboats (some say the permit includes an additional 20 arks), five docks, parking lots, roads, and building upgrades at Waldo Point. (BCDC, Feb 5, 2004 Commission Meeting Notes) For years, Arques worked to complete the requirements of the BCDC permit and comply with Marin County, but progress was so slow that in 1977 he was forced to lease the property to Waldo Point Harbor, a limited partnership whose ultimate goal was to develop and purchase the property. The lease included the ferries *Charles Van Damme* and *San Rafael,* plus Spreckels House, with the intent of renovation and reconstruction if Arques could prove he had title to the vessels. (Garlic press quoting Memorandum Lease, "that certain unrecorded lease," County Recorder's office 1-26-77). The 52-year lease came with an option to buy at any time, which was exercised probably a few years later. (Rose, pers. comm.)

"Nobody expected that the place would change so much once the permits were in place; it was just a detail we had been working at for seven years," a houseboat resident confesses. Shown here, *The Dragon Boat* on Issaquah Dock. Some of the largest and most expensive houseboats (aka floating homes) are on Issaquah Dock.

## Yellow Ferry Harbor

Similar to the beaching of the ferryboat *Vallejo* at Varda Landing, Alexis and Mimi Tellis beached the *City of Seattle* on one of their underwater lots. One story is that they scuttled a barge in the mud to provide access out to the ferry, and ran power lines out to the boat through floating Gallo wine jugs.

Yellow Ferry Harbor with the hills of the Marin Headlands beyond.

The entrance to Yellow Ferry Harbor.

Yellow Ferry Harbor is laid out in a random pattern with winding docks, maximizing views for its tenants

## Kappas Marina

Kappas Marina was the first houseboat marina built, with East and West Kappas docks completed around 1974. Since there were no houseboats (or very few), on the property at the time, construction was not delayed by an established community as it was in the case of Waldo Point Harbor. The marina has a very simple geometric pattern designed to make construction easy and fast. This "Kappas' style development" is what encouraged part of the houseboat community on Arques' property to organize and help develop a less suburban style development.

The houseboats at Kappas Marina.

George Kappas had allowed houseboats in his yacht harbor on the deep water part of his property, and some of these moved to his houseboat marina when he offered the slips to them. Many others went to Waldo Point Harbor when they saw the nature of housing development that had been designed and also because of the deeper water at Waldo Point. As a result, many of the slips were filled with boats built by speculative builders. (Garlic Press, 2-25-75) The need for affordable housing at that time was immediate, so the homes were built as quickly and efficiently as possible. This meant that many of the designs were repeated with slight variations, and simplicity of design was key.

Kappas (aka Steckler-Pacific) also built a shopping center and offices—92,500 square feet office and 7,500 square feet restaurant (DKS Associates, 1983)—at the entrance to his marina. The shopping center exists (it is told) primarily because of the "The Bait Shop," a store that stood in this general area and sold fish and bait for the fisherman when the area was still a shipyard. By continuing the existence of "The Bait Shop," now primarily a convenience store, the shopping center meets the government's requirements for marine use.

Kappas Yacht Harbor (aka Richardson Bay Marina), where many of the original houseboats were berthed, is now a yacht marina and serves as a breakwater for the houseboat harbor.

Small houseboats are tucked into other Richardson Bay marinas.

**The Bait Shop**

It seems contrary to the Public Trust and requirements of BCDC that a shopping center should be within feet of Richardson Bay. According to conversations with one individual who participated in obtaining the permits for the marinas, BCDC maintained that the shopping center could be built if the bait shop (a maritime use) could stay near its Waldo Point location. Today, "The Bait Shop" is primarily a grocery store but stands as a testament of the intent of BCDC. One old advertisement from a copy of the *Sausalito News* in the 1950s describes "FRESH SALMON DAILY at the Bait Shop…Waldo Point."

**Real Estate Prices**

One of the houseboats in Kappas Houseboat Harbor is the *Duchess Blackpool* (Moses, 7-15-96, p. 7), a 66 person lifeboat. According to an old newspaper article, the lifeboat was turned into a houseboat in the 1960s by building a small house on top with a small living room, lower sleeping and living area, a sleeping loft above and a tiny kitchen, bathroom, and shower. One old photo shows a lifeboat with a cabin that sold for $700 in 1970. (Dubin, 1975, p. 17) In 1996, Rick Bernard sold the same kind of houseboat for just under $100,000 when he was selling off a group of boats he had acquired over the years as rentals. The next owner put the boat in a barge, with hopes of later removing the hull and building a "real floating home."

By 1996, houseboats were selling for anywhere between $50,000 and $600,000. Financially, buying a houseboat did not make sense. Realtors sold houseboats based on the concept that you were buying a lifestyle. Retirees and divorcees began buying houseboats because they wanted a change and wanted to live in a community that was safe. Many of the slips provided stunning views. There were around 450 houseboats in Sausalito at that time. Designs ranged from primitive barges to multilevel floating palaces with gourmet kitchens. (Moses, p. 7)

# Commodore Marina

Commodore Marina is close to Kappas by water, but only accessible from Sausalito by getting on and off Highway 101. This small community of houseboats consists of 11 houseboats (17 units total) tucked behind the heliport and is actually located in the town of Mill Valley. The area began as a seaplane base, though some people claim that the houseboats were there first. During the 1950s, the airport was one of the largest flight schools in the area, with 12 aircraft and 140 students. During the 1960s, the building was leased by the Grateful Dead and Jefferson Starship bands for their music studios. Today, it primarily serves as a seaplane base with San Francisco Bay tours and flights to Lake Tahoe. The buildings house commercial and office space. (Price, pers. conv. 2006)

The seaplanes at Commodore Marina.

Commodore Houseboat Marina consists of a small group of boats located around a central dock area.

### The Heliport
Based on the history of the area, it is conceivable, as some say, that this airport may have been built during the war to support the Marin Shipyard. According to one story from the houseboat community, the airport was built to provide air service to Lake Tahoe with daily flights from Sausalito. The history of this area is sketchy, but the site is considered an integral part of the Richardson Bay houseboat communities because it was the location where many of the "illegal" houseboats were hauled out on their way to being destroyed.

Commodore Marina is just over the line between Sausalito and Mill Valley. Nonetheless, most of the houseboaters at Waldo Point and Kappas consider Commodore very much a part of the community.

## Anchor-outs

The rest of Richardson Bay is, for the most part, an open field for boats to anchor in. The term "anchor-out" refers to "a houseboat or live-aboard which is moored or anchored offshore rather than at a marina or shoreside facility." (Richardson Bay Special Area Plan, January 1984) There are still a number of anchor-outs in Richardson Bay, but not in the numbers that existed in the 1970s. The anchor-outs are unauthorized, many "squatting" on public land, and "not a permitted use" according to the Public Trust and BCDC. In the late 1980s, Sausalito and Marin County began removing derelict boats (presumably abandoned) from the bay. In the late 1990s, the *San Francisco Chronicle* claimed that approximately one hundred anchored-out boats were still used as residences (Nolte, 6-7-01). In 2000, as many as sixty were hauled out at the Corps of Engineers Dock and destroyed.

Richardson Bay has numerous boats anchored out, either permanent live-aboards or transient vessels.

An anchor-out from the community's earlier days, still anchored off Waldo Point.

Docks are available for anchor-outs to tie their dinghys to when they come to shore, but for the most part owners need to make arrangements to use someone else's dock while they go ashore.

# Chapter 5
# The Evolution of Houseboat Design and Construction

During the early days of the houseboat communities in Richardson Bay, the term "houseboat" was literally appropriate—a house on a boat. From the late 1940s to the 1970s, the various groups of people settling on the water at Waldo Point typically were not wealthy (or, if they did have financial means, they were looking for a less ostentatious lifestyle). Prevalent at this time were individualistic, communist, democratic, and other philosophies encouraging a particular lifestyle contrary to the popular culture of the era. Reusing materials that others were throwing away seemed to support this counter-culture lifestyle, in which people supported each other—even with differences in background and lifestyle—and worked together to create a peaceful community. In addition, many people in this group were very imaginative, creative individuals, a characteristic perhaps inspired by the desire to excel outside of the conventional rules of the time.

A house built on a lifeboat hull anchored near the multi-million dollar houses on Strawberry.

A house on a steel lifeboat hull, according to some originally from Waldo Point. Now named *Wildflower*, it is berthed in Galilee Harbor.

A house on a World War II balloon barge at Yellow Ferry Houseboat Harbor.

The early houseboat communities consisted of a random group of boats. Here, on South Forty Dock at Waldo Point Houseboat Harbor, are a house on an LCVP (right), a houseboat transferred to a barge (center), a house on a tugboat hull (background, left), and today's newer, larger "floating home" (background, right).

A house built on a World War II landing craft hull.

**What is a "houseboat"?**

The definition of a houseboat varies, depending on one's personal experience. In the Sacramento and San Joaquin river delta, a houseboat can mean a navigable recreation vessel, floated up and down the river. A houseboat in Richardson Bay means a "floating home secured to a pier but not used for navigation." (BCDC Houseboats and Liveaboard Boats, July 1985, Staff Report, p. 6) The Sausalito code defines a houseboat as:

"A boat, vessel or structure in the water, intended generally to be supported by means of flotation and to be maintained without a permanent foundation, used principally for residential purposes and generally not used for active navigation and provided with a city-approved sewer connection." (Sausalito Municipal Code, Ord. 1047, 1, 1989)

The *Pirate* was the home of famous actor and author Sterling Hayden.

## Recycled Hay Scows and Crew Barges

One of the first type of boats to be reused as homes were hay barges and their crew barges. These barges were about 32' x 110' and were originally used to haul hay to San Francisco, when horses were still the primary source of transportation in the city. As many as ten of these barges would be piled with hay, lashed together, and towed down the Sacramento River with a steam tugboat. Along with these tugboats came a smaller barge, typically 16' x 32' that served as galley and crew quarters for the workers on the barge. The hay barges would lay off of Belvedere in the lee of Angel Island and the crew would stay on the crew's quarter barge while they worked to haul the hay barges back and forth to San Francisco and off load the hay. (T. Rose, pers. comm.)

This hay barge was purchased by the wife of architect Bob Anshen and remodeled into a houseboat and apartment. It originally had a 9' tall bilge under the main level and floated. Eventually the bilge was removed and the barge was fixed to pilings driven in the mud.

When automobiles became the main source of transportation, the need for hay barges ended, along with the need for the crew quarters barges. In bayside towns all around San Francisco, these small barges were converted into houseboats or later hauled onto land and turned into houses, offices, and shops, where they were called "arks." Some of the houseboats stayed on the water and were converted into vacation houseboats for wealthy San Franciscans. (Frank, 1977) The hay barges were converted to other uses as well, and eventually many retired as houseboats at Waldo Point. One vintage photo shows as many as six of these hay barges at Waldo Point Harbor during the 1970s.

Ark row on Humboldt in Sausalito. Some have been altered or rebuilt, but for many of these the original barge is still intact on the pilings.

The *Becky Thatcher*, rumored to be original to the Arques Shipyard at Waldo Point, is said to be one of the crew barges for the hay scows. The name "ark" was assigned to this structure in the early 1900s and the name stuck when they were put on pilings for shipyard workers to live in. The term "ark" now refers to a building over the water on pilings. Many of these barges came to Arques shipyard and were used as housing for the workers.

Some of the arks near Main Dock at Waldo Point.

The previous owner of the *Ameer* determined that it was probably one of the houseboats that floated in Belvedere lagoon. The new owner doubled the square footage by putting the home on a concrete basement barge. The *Ameer* is shown here on a foggy day at extreme low tide. When floating, the waterline comes up to the dark line.

Even the Waldo Point Harbor office was once a crew barge. Ted Rose recalls that when he first took over the building to convert it to an office, it had eight tiny rooms, or cabins. This building was one of the original buildings at Waldo Point. Rose recalls discovering a number of these barges during the process of constructing the marina.

A crew barge converted to a houseboat, now an ark on pilings at Waldo Point Harbor.

This ark is located on Main Dock, the original dock to the Arques shipyard at Waldo Point. According to assesor records, it was built in 1900.

The contractor for the marina recalls removing dozens of these buildings. Many were built on crew barges.

The *Mayflower*. Like the *Ameer*, the owner has determined that this was one of the turn-of-the-century houseboats built for the rich to float in Belvedere Lagoon during the summers. (Sweeny, pers. comm.)

Main living area of the *Mayflower*. Everything has been kept in its original condition.

Interior detail of the *Mayflower*.

A bedroom in the *Mayflower*.

The moulding and trim details in the *Mayflower*'s kitchen reflect Victorian design in San Francisco at the turn of the twentieth century.

The plan of the *Mayflower* includes four rooms and a bathroom. The Waldo Point Harbor Office had eight rooms before it was converted from an ark. (Rose, pers. comm.)

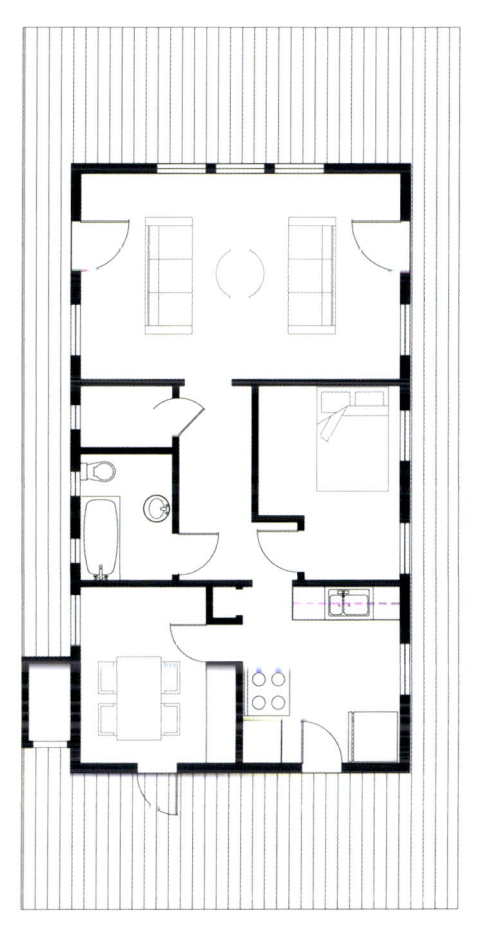

The exterior of the *Mayflower*, with the original porch, typical of the crew barges that were converted to exotic houseboats for the rich at the turn of the twentieth century. These houseboats, not powered, were typically towed into the waters off Sausalito and Belvedere ("Belvedere Lagoon") and anchored. There was no front or back to the vessel and the wraparound porch made it easy to move around the boat for changing views and sun.

Decommissioned hay barges were used to haul other materials for a while, then many retired as houseboats. The floor of the hay barge is constructed to provide the structural strength of the boat. Two layers of two-inch thick tongue and groove planking are laid 90 degrees to each other to form the floor of the barge. Beneath the floor typically was a 9' high bilge (Anshen, pers. comm.), which in most cases was removed for houseboat conversions when the barge was placed on pilings and technically became an "ark." The slight bow of the roof, which also served as a walking deck, sheds water and provides additional structural strength. The exterior walls are canted in slightly.

Before this hay barge became an ark at Waldo Point, it purportedly hauled sand to build the Golden Gate Bridge. Today it is on pilings, has been added on to and reconstructed, and serves as a home and apartment.

Detail of hay barge structure.

Although most hay barges have been transferred to pilings, this one is still floating. The roof has a slight bow, and the walls are canted in slightly. This type of barge was originally used to haul hay to San Francisco at the turn of the century.

Another view of the Appleton Ark. A hot tub sits beneath the circular roof.

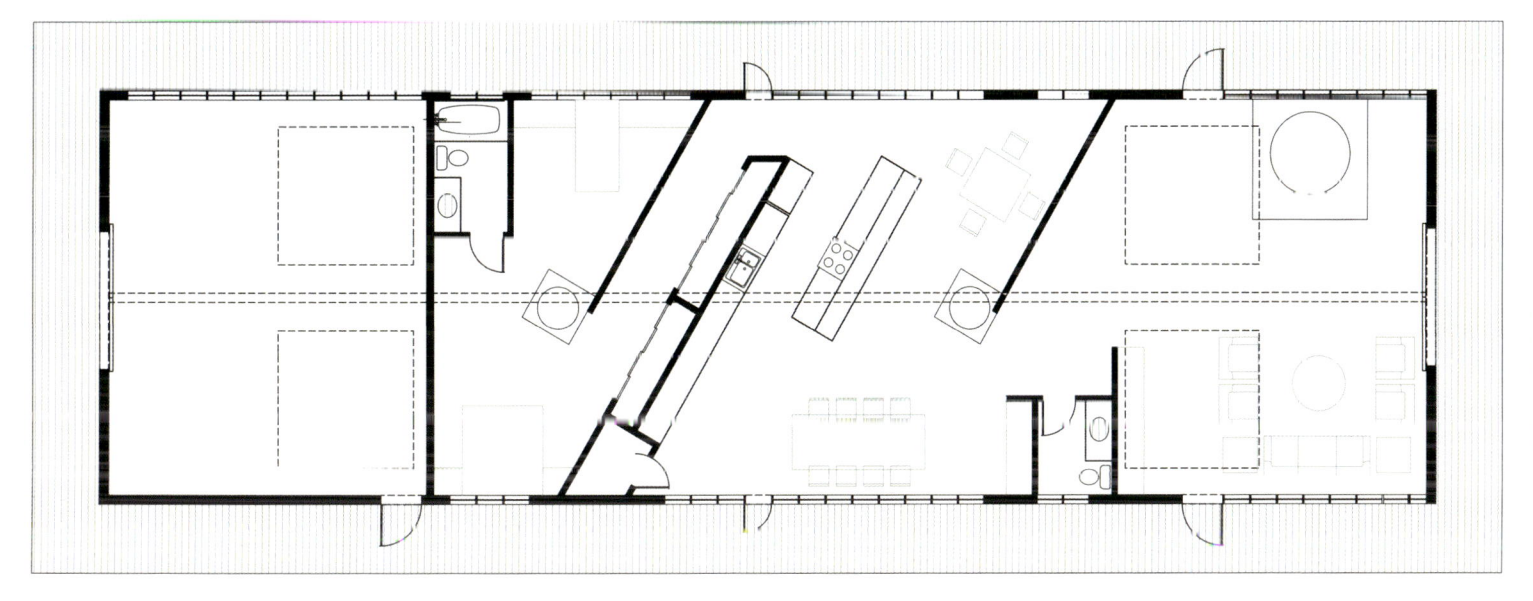

Known as the Appleton Ark, this home grew out of what was originally a hay barge. (Rose, pers. comm.) It started as only a twenty by forty foot structure on the large barge, then slowly grew into the entire barge. It is regarded as one of the best maintained in the marina, and, according to one story, the interior is done entirely in an Egyptian motif.

An example of a hay barge layout. The interior of the barge only had three or four columns down the middle and, like the car deck on the old ferries, it created a wide open, massive space. Many people who used these boats as homes put up only a few walls and curtains, leaving the rest open.

## Decommissioned Ferryboats

In the late 1940s, ferryboats were being decommissioned and sold, and many ended up at the Arques shipyard. The *Vallejo*, The *Issaquah*, The *Clementina*, and others were stripped of valuable equipment, then rented or sold to people as places to live. Many of the ferries had been auto ferries, so the main level was a huge open space, perfect for parties or other community gatherings.

The *City of Seattle*, one of the older wooden ferrys. One story is that she ended up in San Francisco Bay when she was brought back into service to ferry workers to Mare Island during World War II, a common event at the time.

A window was added behind the paddlewheel, according to old photos of the *Vallejo* when it was still operating. The paddlewheel has since deteriorated away.

The *Vallejo* ferried passengers and automobiles beween San Francisco, Mare Island, and Vallejo until 1948. (Dennis, Case, 1977) The autodeck was completely enclosed and a room added to the roof deck.

92

The *Issaquah* ferryboat ran the line from Rodeo to Vallejo over the Carquinez Straits. In 1929, the Carquinez Auto Bridge ended the need for ferry service and the ferryboat *Issaquah*. World War II brought her back into service to bring workers to the Mare Island shipyard. Finally, in 1948, the *Issaquah* was placed out of service, purchased by Arques for $1000, and moved to his shipyard at Waldo Point. Her engine and other valuables were removed and she was then used as a houseboat on Arques' property. (Issaquah Historical Society, 2006) Eventually, she was completely demolished—except for the pilot houses that now stand at the entrance to Galilee Harbor.

What was referred to as the *San Rafael* ferryboat had a similar "decommissioning" as the *Issaquah*. While in service, the *San Rafael* ferried passengers in California from Richmond to San Rafael. The *Clementina*, which is possibly one and the same as what is referred to as the *San Rafael* ferry, was purchased by Don Arques for salvage. According to one account, he let Jon Dane move onto the boat rent free if he would watch the vessel. The *Clementina* was divided into apartments with a few walls and curtains. During the warm months, people lived on the main deck, which was open to the outdoors. (Hoffman, 1976)

The pilothouses from the ferryboat *Issaquah* mark the entrance to the new docks at Galilee Harbor.

This plaque honors the agency that helped to preserve the last remnants of the *Issaquah*, the pilot houses.

93

These ferryboats became an integral part of the community at Waldo Point and Varda Landing, so much so that they were worked into the original plan for the Waldo Point Marina. In one partially approved drawing, "A Composite Plan for the Marin County Houseboat Community" by architect R.P. Young and draftsman J.P. Boeda from 1971, the *Issaquah*, *San Rafael*, and *Charles Van Damme* all have dedicated sites near the shore. The *Charles Van Damme* ferry had the most predominant spot and became the nucleus of the Waldo Point community.

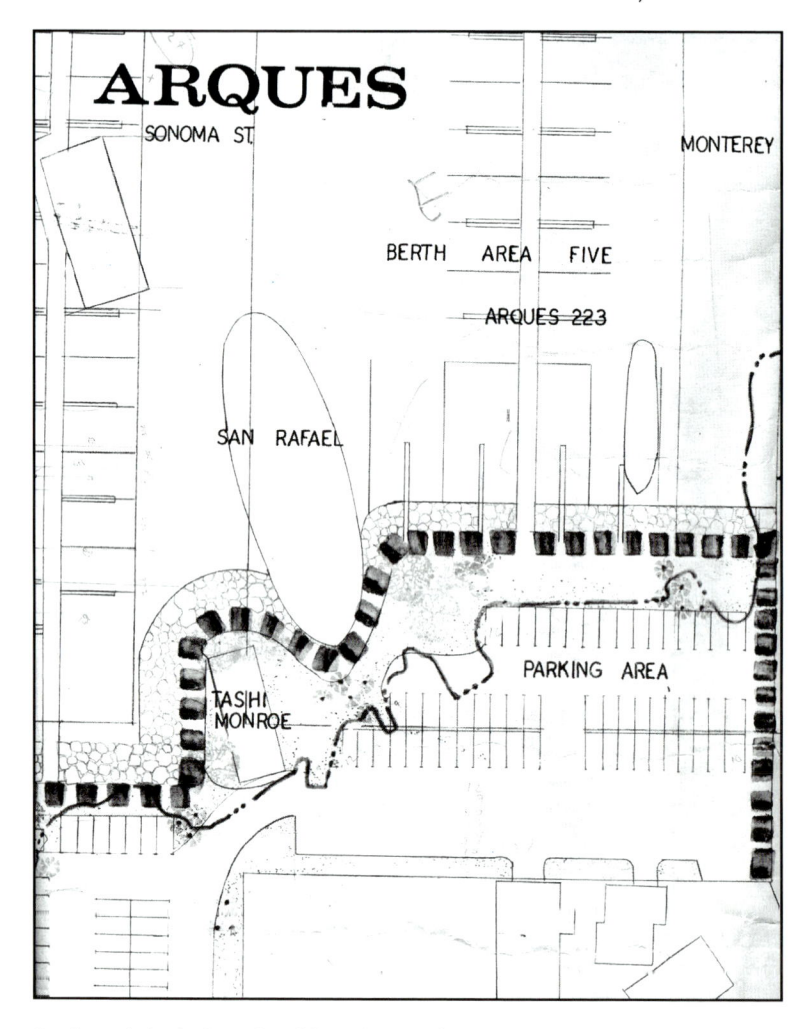

In the original plan of Waldo Point Harbor, the San Rafael ferry had a dedicated location at the south end of the property. It was eventually demolished when the marina was built.

**Charles Van Damme**

The *Charles Van Damme* ferryboat became the "center" of the houseboat community before development. After the boat had gone out of service as a ferry between Benicia and Martinez in the 1950s, it had been reincarnated as the Canton Ferry restaurant, moored outside the city of Oakland. However, the restaurant failed, and Arques saw the opportunity to purchase salvageable material very cheaply. One account claims that he snuck the boat across the bay at midnight with two tugboats and scuttled it on his property by opening its petlocks. Juanita Musson, a restaurateur in Sausalito, offered to rent the *Charles Van Damme* and continue its use as a restaurant. She was able to obtain permission from the Marin County Board of Supervisors to operate as long as she did not discharge raw sewage into the bay. She then dragged it into port in the course of three high tides and beached it on the shoreline. For the price of Coke and sandwiches, the Sea Scouts helped her clean out the lower section where it had been sitting underwater, and she was able to locate an elderly craftsman who had worked on the *Van Damme* in 1913 to help give it a facelift. She even obtained dirt to fill in an area by the boat and create a parking lot. (Hayton-Keeva, 1990)

Juanita was a popular character, and soon the restaurant was frequented by celebrities, including people like Phyllis Diller, Erma Bombeck, Glenn Fort, Jonathan Winters, Tommy and Dick Smothers, and more. (Hayton-Keeva, 1990) There is even a story about the Vienna Boy's Choir appearing one Easter. By 1963, however, Juanita was deeply in debt, most notably to the IRS. A motorcycle gang riot destroyed the interior (*SF Chronicle*, 1963), a drug bust took place, the IRS closed her for back taxes, and, according to Juanita, Arques threatened to sue her over back rent. Juanita told a reporter "that's the end of my mad pad," and, according to one account, the boat was permanently scuttled sometime after that. It then became "The Ark" and was frequented by David Crosby and Dino Valente, and later Stephen Stills, Neil Young, and The Sparrow (later Steppenwolf). (Selvin, 1996)

All that remains of the ferry today is the smoke stack, a partial paddlewheel, and many stories. (Hayton-Keeva, 1990)

All that remains of the *Charles Van Damme* and *Jaunita's* is the smoke stack and a paddlewheel.

The landscape has proliferated around the spot where the *Charles Van Damme* once sat.

## World War II Surplus

After World War II, there was a large quantity of surplus boats that had been built and paid for under contracts with the government, but had never been used. These boats were extremely durable, inexpensive, and easily available.

In 1942, Andrew J. Higgins Industries of New Orleans designed and built various landing craft, including the LCV (Landing Craft Vehicle) and the LCVP (Landing Craft Vehicle, Personnel). These boats were constructed of wood and steel and had the ability to carry fully armed troops, light tanks, field artillery, and other supplies necessary to amphibious operations. They were the boats that made the D-Day landings at Normandy, Guadalcanal, Tarawa, Iwo Jima, Okinawa, and many more. When the war ended in 1945, many were still in production or sitting new in the boatyard. (Strahan, 1998)

After the war, Sausalito Shipbuilding Company (Bob's Boatyard) was appointed dealers and servicing agents for Higgins Industries, builders of these boats. (*Sausalito News,* 1945) It is possible that Sausalito Shipbuilding also became a point to liquidate the unused World War II landing craft from Higgins. This could be why a large quantity of this type of craft ended up in houseboat harbors along the Sausalito waterfront.

Lived in by one of the oldest longtime residents in the community, this LCVP on the Marine Dock in Waldo Point Harbor has solar panels for power and still floats on its original hull.

A Waldo Point Harbor houseboat on an LCVP hull. Many of the houseboats that were built on this type of hull ended up at South Forty Dock in Waldo Point Harbor.

The basic configuration of the Higgins LCVP and LCV made the craft suitable as floatation for a houseboat. It was a shallow draft boat, operating in only eighteen inches of water. It was durable and built to run up on land and over obstacles at full speed without damaging the hull, making it excellent for use on the mudflats in the houseboat harbor during high and low tide. The boat was built to land a platoon of 36 men with equipment or a jeep and 12 men—thus suitable for supporting the weight of a well-balanced house and furnishings on top.

The shape of the bottom, unlike traditional boats, was designed to land a platoon of men and turn around in the surf without broaching—this characteristic could have helped the boat remain stable, even when one or two story houses were built on top of it. The reverse curve of the bottom was planned to protect the propeller and increase speed. When the craft was converted to a houseboat, this reverse curve was used to create a taller ceiling, as a place to hide a waste tank or hot water heater, or as a way to add a bilge pump without taking up valuable floor space. The bow ramp that was added at the request of the Marine Corps for the LCVP made a point of entry onto the houseboat.

Dockside view of a houseboat with twin octagons on an LCVP hull.

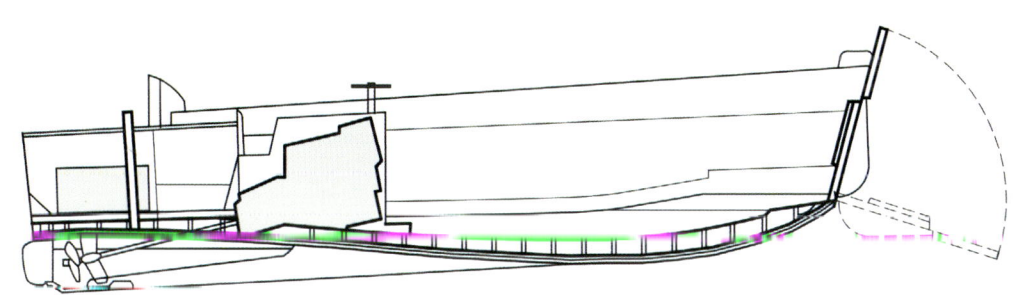

Not only were the LCVP hulls available and cheap, the shape of the hull made it perfect for a houseboat.

97

The waterside view of this houseboat shows how one octagon has been cut away for a skylight.

A free form roof over a 1971 300-square foot single story houseboat on an LCVP hull.

A waterside view of this houseboat. This vintage of houseboat used recycled materials, like windows, siding, and framing from demolished buildings.

The *Pirate Ship* was originally built on an LCVP hull in 1968, according to assessor records. It has since been replaced with a concrete barge.

Dockside view of the same boat.

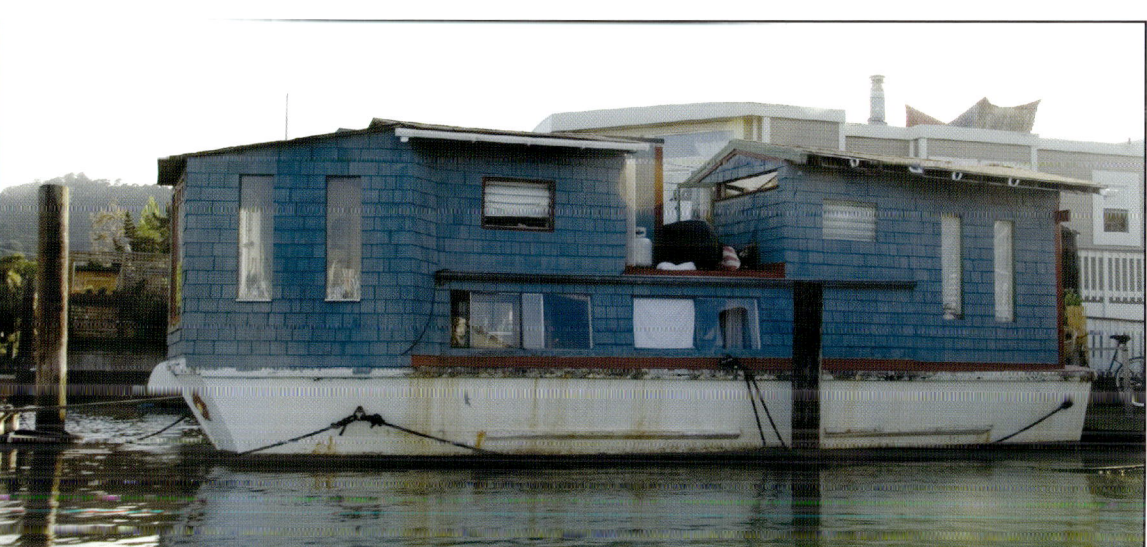

A house on a landing craft hull.

A house on an LCVP hull in Galilee Harbor.

A house on an LCVP hull in Arques Marina.

A two story houseboat on an LCVP.

*Esperanza*. A variation of a houseboat on an LCVP hull.

**LCVP Specifications**

The durable construction of the World War II LCVP made it an ideal flotation for a houseboat:

Construction material: wood (oak, pine, and mahogany)
Displacement 15,000
Length: 36' 3"
Beam: 10', 10"
Draft: 3' aft and 2'2" forward
Speed: 12 knots
Armament: two .30 caliber machine guns
Crew: three (coxswain, engineer and crewman)
Capacity: 36 troops with gear and equipment, or 6,000 pound vehicle, or 8,100 pounds of cargo
Power Plant: Gray 225 HP Diesel Engine

Source: Jerry E. Strahan, *Andrew Jackson Higgins and The Boats That Won World War II*.

Liberty Dock LCVP. The new owner plans to restore the houseboat and hull to their original condition.

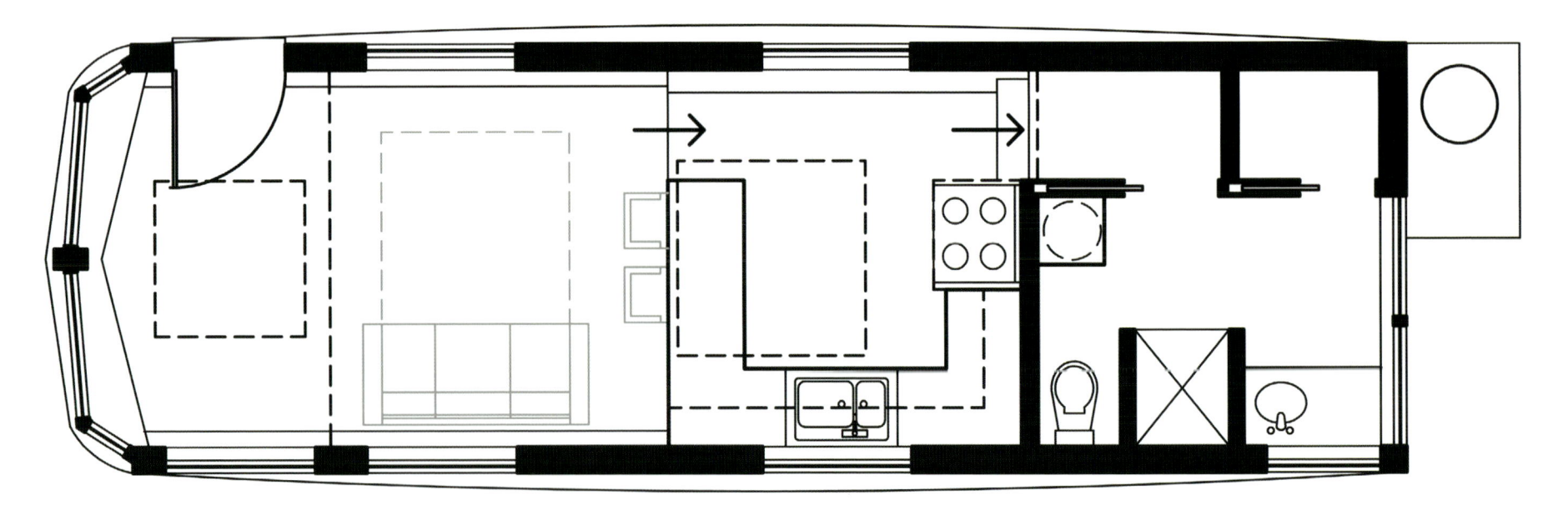

Liberty Dock LCVP. A plan for a houseboat on an landing craft hull currently under construction.

Liberty Dock LCVP.
Skylights bring in light.

Liberty Dock LCVP. Maximum windows give it a panoramic view of the harbor, even though it is in between two larger houseboats

103

The *Lone Star* plan.

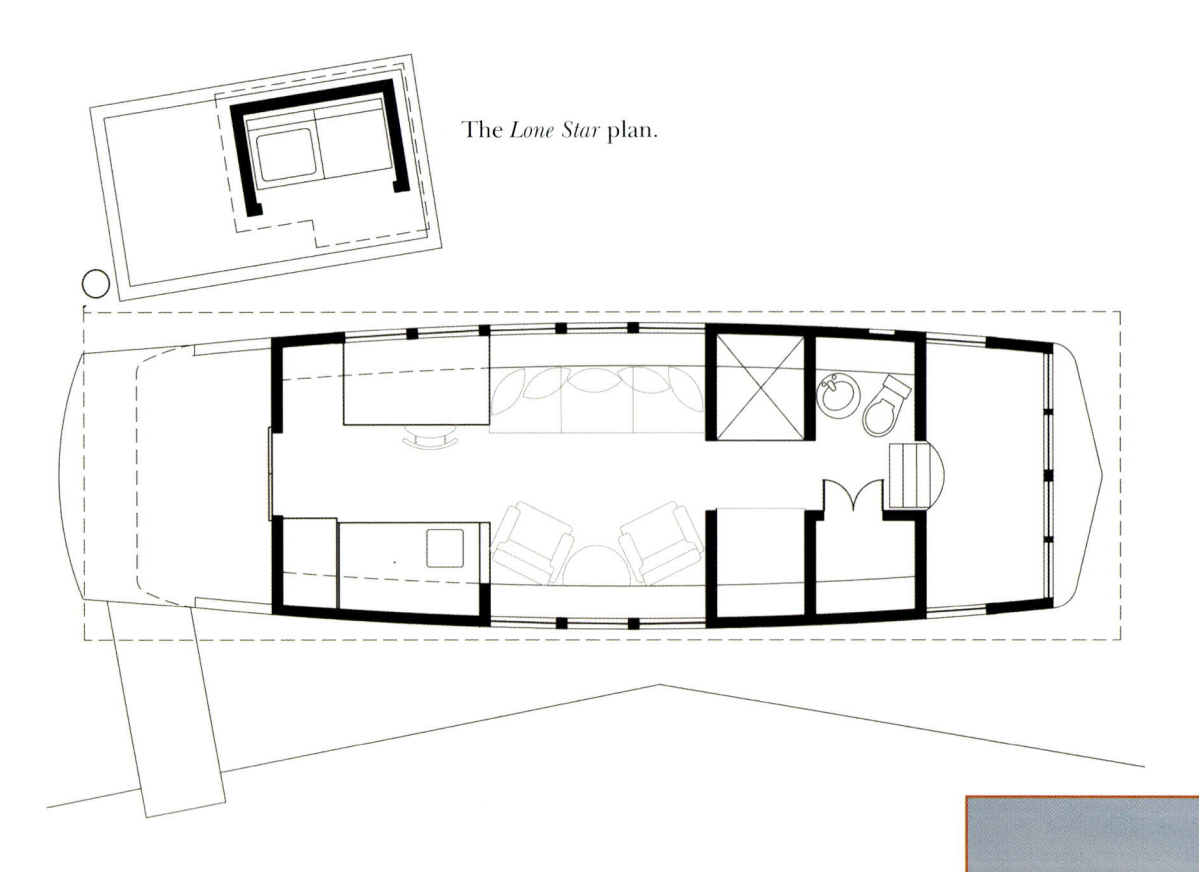

*Lone Star*. The owner recently hauled the boat and repaired and painted the hull.

*Lone Star.* There are a few houseboats that have separate floating barges. This one on the Lone Star is for a washing machine and dryer.

A dockside view of the *Lone Star.*

*Lone Star.* Dishes and utensils are artistically displayed and kept to a minimum.

*Lone Star.* There are only two partitions in the space separating the living area, the bathroom, and the bedroom.

*Lone Star.* A dressing area

*Lone Star.* A bathroom is tucked into a nook.

Art from around the world.

*Lone Star.* A sleeping loft with storage below is in the bow of the boat.

*Lone Star.* The engine and shaft were removed, but the owner kept a piece of the shaft as a momento.

In 1942, Hickinbotham Bros. Constr. Division and Kyle and Company in Stockton, California began building another type of boat under a contract with the Navy and Army Transportation Corp.—the balloon barge. (Dennis and Case, 1977) It is unclear if any of these were ever used during the war. Built out of steel, the boats were 52' long with a large hold. The theory was that the boats would launch large barrage balloons from the hold. They would be attached to a steel cable and anchored to a ring on the deck. The balloons could be raised or lowered to the desired altitude by means of a winch. These balloons served as a type of anti-aircraft system, with the material and mental barrier of a visible cable forcing aircraft to higher altitudes to provide protection from low-level air attacks. (Hillson, 1989)

Less than two dozen of these vessels were built, and at least four of them ended up on the Sausalito waterfront as houseboats. As with the LCV and LCVP, their sturdy wartime construction and displacement area made them capable of supporting the weight of a house. The unique aspect of the balloon barge is the large hold—tall enough for one full level of living space in a houseboat.

Balloon Barge No. 1623 is at Yellow Ferry Harbor.

Balloon Barge No. 1623.

A house built on a World War II balloon barge at Waldo Point Marina was home to Shel Silverstein, famous song writer, cartoonist, and children's book author.

Balloon Barge 1627 was auctioned off in the 1950s, turned into a houseboat in 1959, and is shown as a houseboat in early photos of Arques Marina near where the Sausalito Yacht Harbor is now. When Scott Diamond first saw it, it was called the *Houselight* and moored at Kappas levy. Then, through a series of events, it became derelict. Diamond saw it again in Blackjohn's slough (a Petaluma River tributary) in Novato, remembered it, bought it, and started restoring it. He immediately restored the outside in San Rafael, then found a slip in the Sausalito Yacht Harbor.

Balloon Barge No. 1627 at Sausalito Yacht Harbor, currently under renovation. Most of the characteristics of a balloon barge have been kept intact.

Each balloon barge was given a unique number.

No. 1627. The original door to the engine room. The owner plans to incorporate the door into his design.

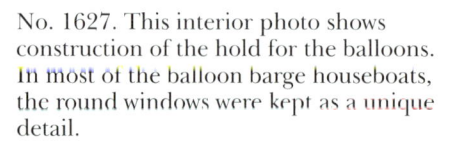

No. 1627. This interior photo shows construction of the hold for the balloons. In most of the balloon barge houseboats, the round windows were kept as a unique detail.

No. 1627. The large steel rings mounted on the deck were used to fly the ballons.

No. 1627. Clerestory windows are added to bring light into the space.

Balloon Barge No. 1624 is in one of the deep water slips on Liberty Dock at Waldo Point Harbor. This two level houseboat is heated with gas fireplaces in each area or room that allow only the room being used to be heated. The roof deck, connected to the main level by a spiral staircase, makes it a full three levels.

Balloon Barge No. 1624, a renovated balloon barge at Waldo Point Harbor.

No. 1624. The entrance to the balloon barge. Minimum alterations were made to the hull.

No. 1624. An exterior view. At one point, the boat was transferred to a concrete hull and windows were cut into the hull.

No. 1624. The main level of the houseboat is completely open. Doors off the dining room lead to a deck. Variations in finished ceiling heights divide the space, and the wooden ceiling gives it the feel of a boat.

No. 1624. Another view of the interior.

113

No. 1624. A spiral staircase leads down to the lower level with two bedrooms and two bathrooms.

No. 1624. An outdoor deck.

No. 1624. A bathroom is tucked into each end of the boat where the hull curves up.

Antisubmarine net buoys were also available and suitable for flotation for a houseboat. The Naval Net (today the Romberg Tiburon Center for Environmental Studies) Depot was located on the east side of the Tiburon Peninsula, a few miles from Sausalito. At this naval base, over 100,000 tons of antisubmarine nets and the buoys to support them were built to protect harbors up and down the West Coast. In the Bay Area, a seven mile long antisubmarine net was stretched across the Golden Gate to prevent Japanese submarines from entering the bay. The nets were anchored by massive concrete anchors and supported by "net buoys," roughly 10 foot diameter steel spheres. When the war was over, these materials were available cheaply, and many of the houseboaters used the unusually buoyant buoys to support their houseboats. For one houseboat at Waldo Point, nine net buoys were able to float roughly a 30 x 30 foot barge with a two story A frame house on it.

This variation on an A-Frame located on the Marine Dock in Waldo Point Harbor originally floated on antisubmarine net buoys before being transferred to a concrete barge.

The Marine Dock A-Frame, from a photo in the Marin County files, shortly after it was transferred to a concrete barge. World War II submarine net buoys that previously supported the boat now float to the side. K. Shaffer 2006.

The master bedroom portion of a two part houseboat on the Yellow Ferry Harbor dock still floats on net buoys. The main house had originally floated on net buoys, but they were replaced with a concrete basement barge to add square footage. The net buoy's sturdy steel construction does not appear to have degraded significantly in the Yellow Ferry houseboat, and the owner plans to keep this historic detail.

Another indication of the durability of these buoys is found in a detail from the Anshen hay barge at Mays Harbor. Anshen had one of Arques' associates, a talented and well-liked individual in the Arques Shipyard named Lindsey Cage, build her a fireplace out of a net buoy. Though unavailable for photographing, this working fireplace is an appropriate example of the ability to translate a piece of outdated equipment into a working piece of equipment, purely for functionality and not as a whimsical adaptation.

Yellow Ferry houseboat, c.1979. This two boat houseboat originally floated on net buoys. The main house was transferred to a concrete barge basement, probably in the late '70s, while the master bedroom suite still floats on the buoys.

The spherical net buoys are nearly hidden from view, giving the houseboat the appearance of floating above the water.

117

A Dutch door serves as the main entrance.

The home is partially heated with a wood stove.

Stained glass in the powder room.

118

The dining area.

The kitchen is located in the narrow point of the diamond.

A clerestory "tower" element is in the middle of the space. Old photos indicate this was once a sleeping loft.

One of the showers is lined with varnished wood.

Leaded glass over the bathtub in the master bedroom suite.

The master bedroom is in a separate houseboat a few steps from the main houseboat.

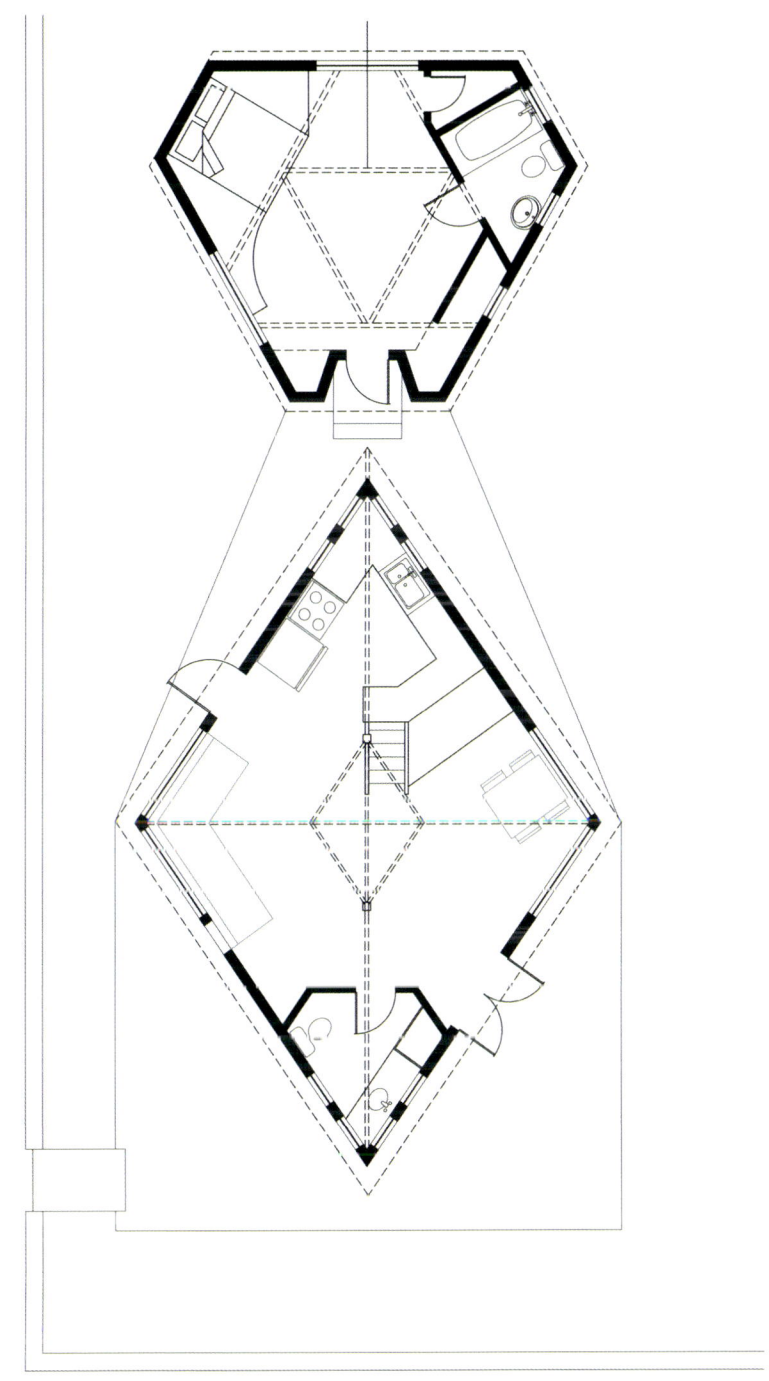

121

Military housing originally built for workers in the shipyards was also available for anyone who could move it. Known for its lightweight, inexpensive construction, this housing was easy to move and float on foam or wood flotation. The houseboat shown here in Yellow Ferry Harbor was once temporary military housing during World War II on Mare Island. (Tellis, pers. comm.)

**Army Barracks Barge**

After the war, Arques purchased an old World War II barracks barge and brought it to Waldo Point Harbor from the Mare Island Naval Base station. He floated the two story building onto his property and planned to use it as apartments. However, the Marin County building inspector would not allow this, so Arques decided to salvage what he could, demolish the building, and reuse the barge. He offered one of his tenants the opportunity to live on the barge rent free while demolishing it. As time went by, the tenant slowly burned parts of the building in a stove on the barge, until all that was left was the barge itself. (Van Loan, 1992) (Diamond, pers. comm.)

This houseboat is documented with a 1957 construction date (probably the date of conversion to a houseboat) and is said to be a house from World War II military housing at Mare Island. New plans are being proposed to replace it entirely with a modern, larger houseboat that utilizes the existing barge.

## Barges and Other Boats

The list of other kinds of reused boats is long—it includes tugboats, riverboats, fishing boats, and old decommissioned ships. Some, like the fishing boats, were working vessels that retired when the owner retired.

A Galilee Harbor wooden sailing vessel as a houseboat.

*Mirene*, a tugboat converted to a houseboat, is the home of the founder, editor, and publisher of *The Whole Earth Catalog*. Many believe that it is the only navigable vessel in the marina.

*Santa Lucia*, once a fishing boat, is now located in Galilee Harbor. According to a tour of Galilee Harbor in 2006, it was "built in 1972 by W.R. Bishoff at Sausalito Marinship," probably referring to the shipyard at Gate 3, where some of the original residents were located before they began Galilee Harbor. (anon., pers. comm.)

*Liberty*, an old boat in Galilee Harbor, possibly a tugboat, was once lived in by a Marin County Supervisor and it is rumored, one of the founders of Antenna Theater, which went on to become Antennae Audio, the leading international company specializing in audio tours.

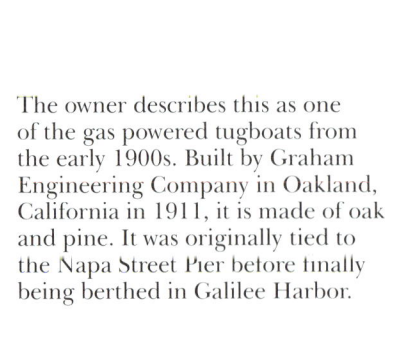

The owner describes this as one of the gas powered tugboats from the early 1900s. Built by Graham Engineering Company in Oakland, California in 1911, it is made of oak and pine. It was originally tied to the Napa Street Pier before finally being berthed in Galilee Harbor.

*Liberty* as seen from Sausalito. She recently suffered fire damage, but rumored plans are to restore her to her original houseboat condition.

Galilee Harbor describes this boat as a "Bay scow…built in 1910 for duck hunting on the Delta." Others say it was a sailing "hay scow" (Dennis, Case, 1977) with the cabin modified taller to make it more livable as a houseboat. The shape of the hull tends to give it more of the appearance of a sailing hay scow from the turn of the century, but, like most houseboats, its actual history is hard to determine because of the age of the boat.

The side windows on the scow-houseboat.

The *Ritz* is described by the owner as a Delta Cruiser built in 1972. "Delta cruisers" come in many shapes and sizes and are factory or homebuilt (like this one, per Galilee Harbor literature). They are typically used as pleasure vessels to cruise the Sacramento and San Joaquin river deltas. This one has been converted to a permanent home.

The hull of this boat was built in 1900, according to assesor records. A house was added later, then subsequently put in a concrete hull. The back of the boat has been cut away to expose the heavy timber construction of the hull and one of the bulkheads that supports the house.

S.S. *Maggie*. Assesor records indicate that this boat was built in 1889, probably referring to the hull, which has the characteristics of a tugboat hull. The houseboat had 1080 square feet of living space and 530 square feet of deck.

S.S. *Maggie*. The back deck.

S.S. *Maggie*. A waterside view.

**The Golden Gate**
   Old barges were cheap and readily available. One resident, who now lives on a balloon barge in Sausalito Yacht Harbor, recalls the story of his barge. In 1970, he bought a 700 ton dredger, the *Golden Gate*, up in Novato. It had twelve-foot ceilings, five bedrooms upstairs, and a galley. "You could fit a 50' sailboat inside the boat downstairs." He took it over to Strawberry Point (across from Waldo Point) to work on it, and when it came up to summer solstice high tide he brought it up on beach as far as it could go so he could continue working on it. The tide went out, and the barge was stuck there for six months. Another barge was moved in from Gate 6, and a few months later a third barge moved in—a 110 foot barge with three families living on board ("very crusty characters"). Eventually, Marin County forced all of the barges to leave, including him, in part because they did not have occupancy permits for the boats. (Diamond, pers. comm.)

The old wooden lumber schooner, *Lassen*, was beached at the foot of Johnson Street in the 1950s and is still talked about today. A beautiful wooden sailing vessel, it was home to artists for many years. (Tracy, 1993, p.171) The boat decayed away, and now all that can be seen at low tide are the remnants of the steel fuel tanks and other metal parts.

The *Yolo*. Records at the County of Marin offices indicate this was originally a navigable wooden hulled river freighter. Originally located in Yellow Ferry Harbor, it is now located at the end of A Dock at Waldo Point Harbor. It has gone through several renovations, including transfer to a concrete barge in 1992. Because of the size of the vessel, a larger than normal barge was built, 25' x 69'. Currently, plans are being made to demolish the *Yolo* and build one of the largest houseboats, or floating homes, in the marina. (Gimmler, March 14, 2005)

A tugboat from the turn of the twentieth century, now a houseboat on South Forty Dock in Waldo Point Marina.

## Buildings and Trailers

Arques did not hesitate to purchase buildings that were scheduled to be demolished and move them to his property. Today, many of the buildings at Gate 3 are just such buildings, but most buildings of this type at Gate 5 are gone. One building that was originally located at Gate 5 was the Spreckels House.

The history of the Spreckels House is sketchy, but according to one account the building was originally constructed as the Pacific Yacht Club clubhouse on the cove near the foot of Main Street. In Sausalito the club faded out of existence in 1899 and the building and land were purchased by John and Adolph Spreckels as a summer house. (Tracy, 1993) At some point, the building was divided into three apartments, and in the 1950s it was scheduled for demolition and replacement with a large apartment building. It was then that Arques purchased the building and towed it to his property at Gate 5 to use as an apartment-boat building there. Arques doubled the number of apartments and began renting it out without any difficulty. Many people remember renting rooms in the Spreckels House; one resident who was born at Gate 3 in Sausalito recalls the story of her sister being born in a pink four-poster bed at the Spreckels House. (Bradley, pers. comm.)

One houseboater even purchased the real estate sales office from Redwood City and floated it across San Francisco Bay to a mooring at Mays Harbor.

This houseboat was originally the sales office for Redwood City south of San Francisco. A neighbor recalls the story of how the owners, during a calm day, floated it under the Bay Bridge, across San Francisco Bay, and into its current location at Mays Harbor.

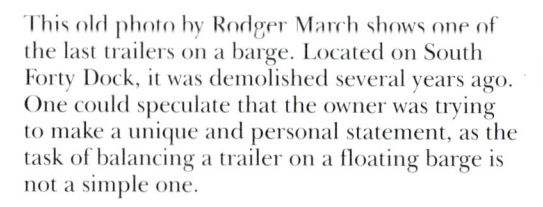

This old photo by Rodger March shows one of the last trailers on a barge. Located on South Forty Dock, it was demolished several years ago. One could speculate that the owner was trying to make a unique and personal statement, as the task of balancing a trailer on a floating barge is not a simple one.

## The Artists

In the 1960s, artists like Chris Roberts and Barney West came to the community. Some came to be close to the teachings of Alan Watts' spiritual philosophies at Varda Landing, and others may have stayed after attending a party at Jean Varda's ferry. Some who came to attend school in San Francisco found the Sausalito houseboats an affordable place to live.

One of the oldest residents in the Richardson Bay houseboat community tells the story of how Chris Roberts was one of Jean Varda's favorite aspiring artists and had an enormous amount of potential. Roberts took very thin, flexible siding (similar to T-111 siding today) and shaped it into fantastic sculptures that could be lived in. One, the "Madonna and Child," was built around a pile driver. Roberts wrapped the frame with material and created a whimsical series of arches and three dimensional curves. Inside, he kept the platforms, and used them as a place to sleep or for people to stay when they needed a place to "crash." When Marin County began cracking down, they wanted to demolish the Madonna because it was not "habitable."

The "Madonna and Child" was a houseboat sculpture built around a pile driver similar to this one. Thin siding was formed around the structure to create a curved sculpture. (Dubin, 1975, cover) The platforms were used to sleep on. Though people stayed in it, it was technically not a houseboat. It burned down in the 1970s.

Chris Roberts' "The Owl" has the same curved lines as the "Madonna and Child."

A detail on "The Owl."

View of "The Owl" from the water.

132

One story frequently told is that Roberts was able to successfully argue that the "Madonna and Child" was a sculpture, and not a houseboat, and should be allowed to stay. Roberts went on to build "The Owl," and was trying to obtain funding to develop the abandoned dry-docks in Richardson Bay into a community center. Unfortunately, he became addicted to drugs, which, some say, led to his death (though others still believe he is alive). In the mid-70s, the "Madonna and Child," at that point an icon in the houseboat community, was "unexpectedly consumed by flames." "The Owl" remains today.

### Barney West

In the 1960s and '70s, Barney West established a studio to create his signature Tiki sculptures at the foot of Napa Street near the site of the Napa Street Pier. The place became known as "Tiki Junction" and there he carved large Tiki sculptures out of huge chunks of redwood with chainsaws and axes. West was a former South Pacific seaman, traveling to places like Bora Bora, Tahiti, Easter Island, and the Marianas. From these travels, he brought back an inspiration to create his interpretation of this style of art. (Klien, 8-6-05) West lived at Tiki Junction in a train car and was quite a recognizable character, with an eye patch and Greek sailing cap. He died in 1981 at the age of 62. (Klien, Marin IJ, 8/6/05)

West's sculptures can now be found in Trader Vic's, a popular Polynesian restaurant, and other stores around the Bay area. One 8-foot statue is supposedly erected at Redwood High School in Larkspur, California. Like many of the artists in Sausalito, West also built a houseboat, which is moored in the Sausalito Yacht Harbor. Known as the *Wooden Shoe*, its signature detail was the second story sleeping loft with inward angled windows at one end of the boat. This detail brought light into the home while maintaining privacy. The stained glass windows, according to one story, were contributed by Ned Martin after he purchased it in the late 1960s. (Rude, pers. comm.)

This scupture, done by another tiki artist, marks the location where Barney West had his outdoor studio on Mono Street, between Marinship and Sausalito. It is said that West's Tiki sculptures can be found throughout California, including one at a high school in Larkspur, California.

A waterside view of the *Wooden Shoe*. Some believe the name, passed down over the years, references the shape of the boat.

133

Many of the houseboats built during the 1960s and '70s can be viewed as people's artistic expression encapsulated in a house. Art and creativity extended beyond the houseboat and into decoration. Some of the old artwork has remained, and new artwork has been added over time.

Gretchen Metzger, an artist who lives in Mill Valley, created this paper sculpture that decorates a stairway in one of the LCVP houseboats.

A sculpture on the back deck of *Lone Star* by Ruby Neri.

A carved sculpture on the South Forty Dock at the entrance to *Vichychoisse*.

A colorful scupture.

A stained glass landscape.

A mural on the side of a building at the entrance to Galilee Harbor.

135

A raft with two carved seals frames the entrance. Some say this is used as a "porch," Unpowered, it is anchored in place and visited by dinghys.

A whimsical seahorse sculpture.

A sculpture in the *Lone Star* by Ruby Neri. The original frame of the boat is still visible.

A teapot as a mailbox.    Sculptures and siding variations.    A colorful stair in in Luna di Miele at Yellow Ferry Harbor

## Recycled Wood And Building Material

Many of the houseboats were built from wood and material recycled from buildings that were being demolished. In the 1950s and '60s, the construction of urban renewal projects, airports, transportation projects, or simply newer, more stylish buildings led to the demolition of existing historic houses and buildings. One resource of Victorian artifacts came when large areas of nineteenth century Victorian homes were demolished in the Western Addition in San Francisco as part of federally-sponsored urban redevelopment projects.

A few nineteenth century residences were moved to Beideman Place, Eddy, and Scott Street during the consruction fo the Western Addition. The rest were demolished and the remains sold at salvage shops.

One resident recalls how "they stripped out a three block by ten block area of old Victorians, and in the process drove one of the minority communities out of San Francisco…there were a number of places on McAllister Street called the McAllister Street bandits that had sheds full of stained glass for five bucks apiece and solid redwood doors for three dollars… an awful lot of the stuff that went into the houseboats came out of there." (anon.)

138

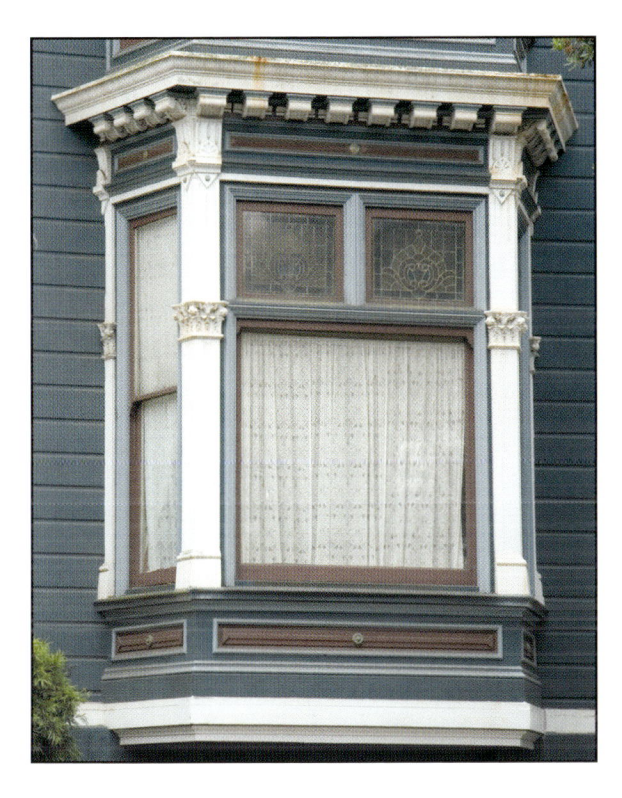

A leaded glass window on one of the houses on Biedeman Place.

When the Victorians in San Francisco were torn down to build the Western Addition, pieces of stained glass were cheap and easy to buy at salvage shops.

Even basic wood windows were salvaged.

Sterling Hayden was trying to recreate the look of a riverboat on a tugboat hull around the time the Western Addition was being razed. (Dennis, Case, 1977) Many materials on boats at this time were salvaged from these buildings.

A detailed front door from one of the moved rescued houses.

Other areas with Victorian homes in San Francisco were demolished as a result of highway projects. This provided a tremendous resource for ornate columns, windows, doors, fireplaces, and stained glass. It was not until the late 1960s that San Francisco adopted a landmarks ordinance to prevent the further demolition of these historic neighborhoods. (San Francisco Preservation Society, 2003) One houseboat that was originally a hay barge was finished completely with redwood from a house that was torn down to build the San Jose Airport. (Anshen, pers. comm.) As with the recycled boats, many of the people who were reusing materials from demolished houses were doing so out of principle rather than necessity. The idea of perfectly usable materials being "thrown away" was considered irresponsible to many.

The interior of this houseboat was finished with salvaged wood from a house that was being torn down to build the San Jose Airport.

*Clamshell* in Yellow Ferry Harbor. The owner, who acquired the boat in 1976, describes this as a boat using all recycled materials. Parts came from Mare Island shipyard, Marin barns and fences, and an arch from a Mission district church. The stained glass doorway came from a store in Haight-Ashbury, and the loft ceiling from a chicken house in Petaluma. (Sexton, 1989) The houseboat is about 1200 square feet and is on a concrete basement.

The windows in this houseboat at Mays Harbor were reclaimed.

A sleeping loft above the kitchen in the Mays Harbor houseboat. One resident from the seventies recalls how a barge carrying lumber and building supplies was on its way west, and when it got outside the Golden Gate, it wrecked and lost most of its lumber. "Everyone went out there and was picking up brand new unused lumber…some of it in bundles." (March, pers. comm.)

The Clamshell

142

When Arques' attorney and Marin County wrote the houseboat code in the late 1960s, they tried to bring in the fire and electrical safety provisions of the Uniform Building Code but also add in parts to encourage the use of alternative materials, in part because that was what was available. The residents involved in writing the code felt they had to protect that process of alternative construction, and including it in the local code gave it credibility. This was enforced for a number of years. (anon, pers. comm.)

Irregular doors on a houseboat in Galilee Harbor.

Barney West's *Wooden Shoe*. (Rude, pers. comm.) Originally it had a three-hundred year old St. Elizabeth, a tiny piece of real Tiffany, and pieces salvaged from an urban renewal prject in Pittsburgh. (Dennis, Case, 1977) The Tiffany and St. Elizabeth have since been removed but some of the others remain.

143

## The Introduction of the Lifeboat Hull

The late 1960s brought one of the largest influxes of youth to San Francisco and the community exploded, but reusing boats and building houses on them was still popular. Piro Caro described these people to a *New York Times* reporter as the "lost children of the middle class." When a merchant ship and its equipment was being decommissioned up the Delta, Forbes Kiddoo saw an opportunity buy the lifeboats off the ship and sell them to the "kids" at Waldo Point. (Kiddoo, pers. comm.) The deep hull and large displacement was perfect to build a house on. A few are still in the marina, though many have had their hulls removed or are scheduled for total replacement.

---

**Where Did the Lifeboats Come From?**

A large number of lifeboats came to Waldo Point, but few remain today. Some attribute this to the quality of the hulls. According to one story, in the 1960s, the International Maritime Organization (IMO) outlawed a particular kind of lifeboat because of its cheap construction. These were lifeboats that were on the freighters from World War II. Before there were any permits required, Forbes Kiddoo and his partner would pick up these decommissioned lifeboats and tow them over to Waldo Point—"six in a row" some say—and sell them to people there who wanted a place to stay. The lifeboats were outfitted with a sailing mast, sails, and water jugs (but the metal was very thin). "You could set the mast up and drape the sail over it and live there from that night on." One resident claims that Kiddoo brought as many as two hundred lifeboats to Waldo Point. Whether that number is accurate or not, the availability of these hulls could be connected to the population explosion on Arques' property at Waldo Point. (anon., pers. comm.)

---

A lifeboat hull for a houseboat anchored off of Waldo Point.

An anchored out houseboat built on a lifeboat hull.

A 1970s houseboat in an old lifeboat hull, now in a concrete barge.

This houseboat in Gates Cooperative at Waldo Point Harbor grew out of what appears to be a lifeboat hull.

145

*Caribe* was described as a "26' cemented houseboat" (Koestel, 1995) before it was moved off the property in 1994 during the W.P. Gates Cooperative Fill Reduction Project. K. Shaffer 2006

*St. Brendan Cloud*, a house on a lifeboat, was demolished in 1993. K. Shaffer 2006

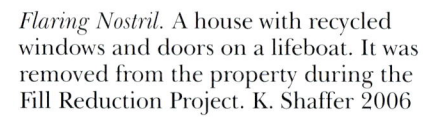

*Flaring Nostril*. A house with recycled windows and doors on a lifeboat. It was removed from the property during the Fill Reduction Project. K. Shaffer 2006

Known as *Santasmagoria* and *Butterfly* at Waldo Point in the 1960s and 1970s. K. Shaffer 2006

internationally known artists, musicians—basically people with the means to live anywhere no matter what the cost—all coming to hide in the houseboat community. For people performing in San Francisco, a twenty minute drive from the city brought them to a completely isolated community. Otis Redding was one of those who came to hide out on Main Dock at Waldo Point after being harassed by fans in the city. (Selvin, 1996)

A Kappas West houseboat from the 1980s. K. Shaffer 2006

There are a variety of documented histories of the migration to California from the East Coast during the 1960s and '70s. Among the longtime residents in the communities along Richardson Bay are people from states such as New York, Ohio, Pennsylvania, and Rhode Island, to name a few. Most came looking for a change from the traditional lifestyles in their original locations. The documentary called *Berkeley in the Sixties* chronicles the specific sequence of events that attracted people to the Bay area. One story is told by Ellen Schlesinger in her article for the *New York Times*, "You Call this Living?" Schlesinger and her husband, along with a trust fund, came to Berkeley looking for a change in lifestyle. Seeking a place to live that was more "mellow" than Berkeley, they ended up in the houseboat community (at Waldo Point) on what she described as a "redwood houseboat." A guitarist for Janis Joplin was one neighbor, another had lived with the Grateful Dead. (Schlesinger 1976)

Many of the residents tell stories of neighbors that were trust fund babies, children waiting for an inheritance (the heir to the Anheuser-Busch fortune is featured in one story), actors, movie producers,

The owner calls this the *Guy Lombardo* (Flanagan, 2004); it is also known as the "Potato Chip" boat to some local residents. One local story tells how the original owner designed the roof to cut the winds that came down the hills from Sausalito.

*Rosalia* in Galilee Harbor, built on a lifeboat hull.

Layout of a lifeboat on Liberty Dock, at one time known as the "*Duchess Blackpool*…a 66 person lifeboat from the Kaiser Shipyards" in the *Marin Independent Journal* on July 13, 1996. In 1996, the owner sold it for just under $100,000 when he was "selling off the fleet" of houseboats he had amassed and used as rentals.

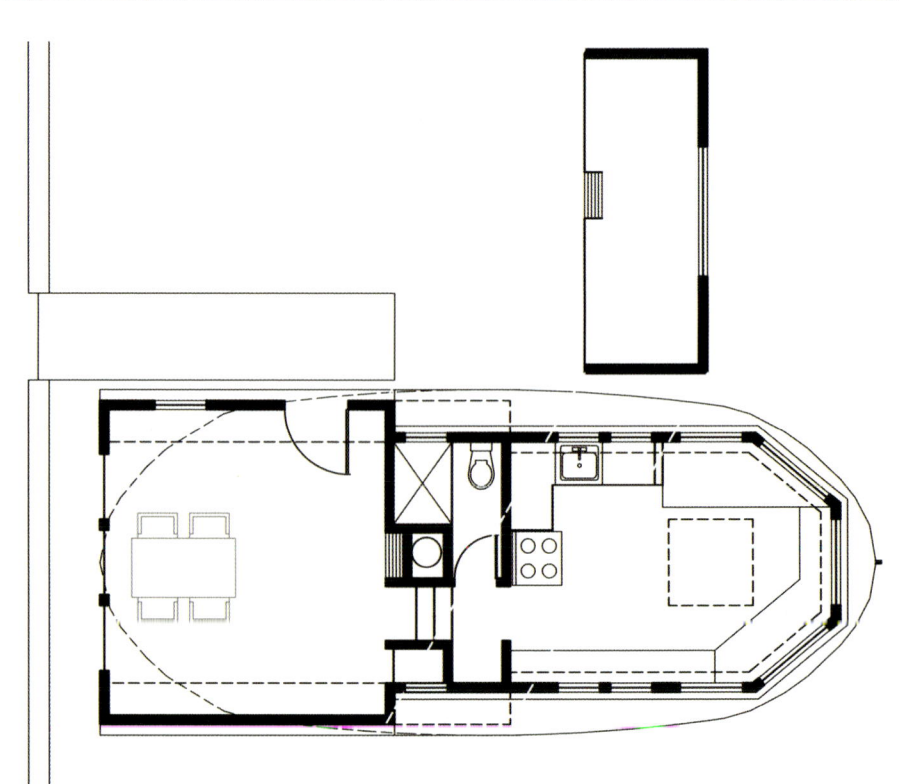

148

# The A-Frame and Other Small House Designs

The A-frame design was also a popular houseboat/floating home design during the early days of the houseboat community, for several reasons. The design made it more rigid while floating in the water, it did not take a lot of material, and it was easy for one person to build. Not very many are left today.

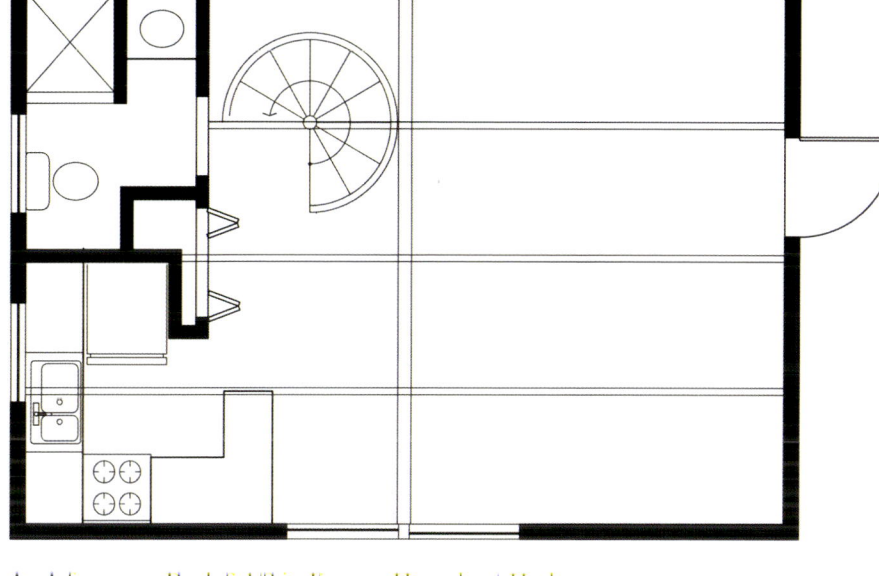

An A-frame on Dock 6 1/2 in Kappas Houseboat Harbor.

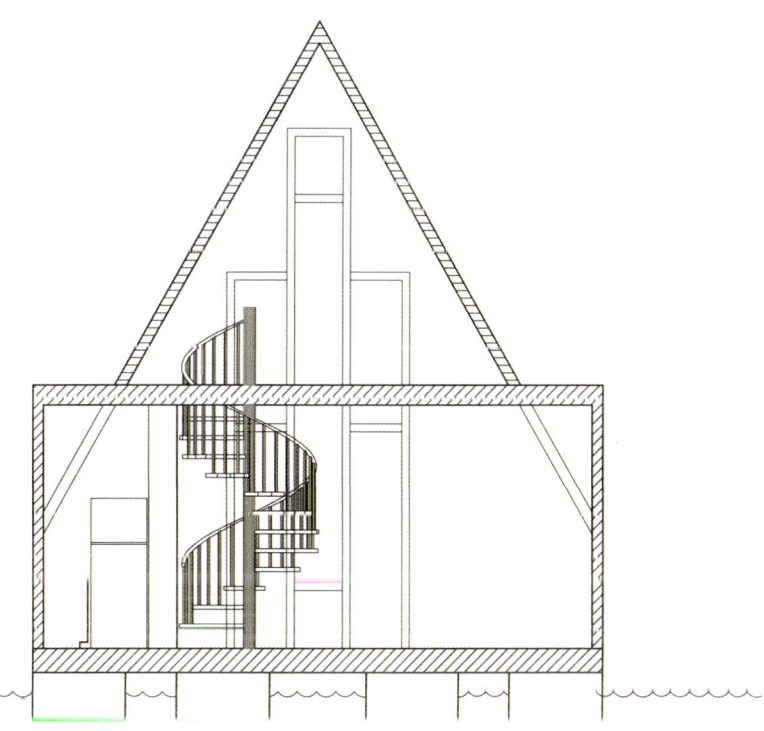

An A-frame in Yellow Ferry Harbor.

Section of the A-frame on Dock 6 1/2. Today, this boat would probably not meet code; among other issues, it is too wide and has too much glass to meet the California Energy Code.

Other small houses were built, typically on Styrofoam, and usually less than 400 square feet. Many of these original designs are located on South Forty Dock and were built from recycled materials.

A small, detailed, and efficient houseboat. A small house was easy for someone to build on their own.

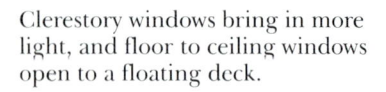

Clerestory windows bring in more light, and floor to ceiling windows open to a floating deck.

Comprised of less than 400 square feet of living space, including a deck, this houseboat is a year round residence. Like many of the small houseboats, its materials were recycled from other building projects.

A 200 square foot fully functional houseboat. The water heater and entrance are protected from prevailing northwest winds and the windows are maximized on the south and east to add light and bring in solar heat.

**Drugs**

By the early 1970s, the community had increased in size significantly and other counter-culture influences, such as the increasing popularity of illegal drugs, were having an effect. Stories abound regarding drug deals, drug parties in the Bay at low tide, drug busts at the Trident (a popular bar and restaurant in Sausalito), and vendetta killings at the Howard Johnson's just outside of Sausalito, not to mention drug overdose related deaths. There is some documentation, plus credible sources, to indicate that many of these stories are true, although some have certainly been embellished.

Some theorize that this influence caused many people to leave the community, while others came and stayed in order to be close to their trusted supplier. One long time resident expresses her dissatisfaction with this time period, as the careers of many extremely talented artists were destroyed due to addiction.

## The Abatement Of The Ferries At Waldo Point

In the spring of 1971, apparently in response to complaints from Marin County's more affluent residents who were disgusted by the unconventional lifestyle and architecture at Waldo Point, Marin County supervisors authorized Richard Larson, the marine inspector, to tow away six houseboats for demolition. Four of the six houseboats were occupied (Marinscope, 5-25-71), one by contractor Harold Holzinger of Corte Madera. This step made it apparent that Marin County was serious about regulating the community and getting rid of the non-traditional houseboats. However, many of the residents at Waldo Point organized and resisted the abatement. (Nolan, Rouda, 1974) Marin County then decided to try redevelopment instead. A plan was approved to build houseboat marinas on Kappas' property and Arques' property in 1971. Eventually, in 1976, when Arques still had not finished developing Waldo Point Marina, Marin County officials threatened him with fines and imprisonment until he finally agreed to lease his property to a real estate development company who promised to develop the property over the next two years. (Ledbetter, 3-14-1977) When this happened, one style of houseboat that was immediately under threat of abatement was the ferry.

According to an interview between a reporter for *The Garlic Press* and Piro Sanchez, the "town philosopher" for Waldo Point, by 1966 the dispute between Marin County and Arques had reached a breaking point. Up until then, Arques had insisted he would clean up the property if Marin County would issue him permits, but the county would not issue permits because that would be interpreted as legal recognition of the houseboat community. Arques was charged with "Maintaining a Hazardous Nuisance," referring to the houseboat community, and he agreed to let the county come on his property and clean it up at "public expense" for six months. The terms of the agreement included the razing of sixty hulls down one foot below the mudline (probably an impossible task), including Piro Sanchez' home, the *San Rafael* ferry.

The *San Rafael* ferry had been retired in 1956 when the Richmond Bridge was built. Lindsay Cage and Jerry Kolfuss bought her for salvage, brought her to Arques' property, and removed the engine. They sold what was left to a restaurateur, who abandoned it there. One day, a young fourteen-year-old boy, like many who came to the houseboat community, asked Piro where he could find a place to live as he could no longer live with his family. Piro sent him to Don Arques, who let him live on the ferry. The boy lived there for a few years, Sterling Hayden used the boat as a writing studio for a while, and then later, when Piro was forced to move out of his houseboat in Belvedere, he moved into the *San Rafael* ferry. The story continues that Piro paid the back rent for the restaurateur who had left it there and thus officially became owner of the boat. When Marin County threatened to raze the boat in their action against Don Arques, Piro defended his home.

Arques did work to develop a permitable plan for the community, and the *San Rafael* was worked into this plan, along with the other ferryboats. In the end though, presumably because the developers did not see a financial benefit to maintaining them, all the ferry boats at Waldo Point Harbor were eventually demolished. The last remnants of the *San Rafael* ferry, the pilot houses that had been put on a barge, were documented as being demolished in 1993-95 as part of a fill reduction project by Gates Cooperative for BCDC. The only ferries that were preserved were privately owned.

All that was left from the *San Rafael* ferry were the wheel houses, as shown in this Gates Coop photo from the WPH Gates Cooperative Fill Reduction document. *Courtesy Ted Rose.*

## Sanitary Systems

In the early days of the houseboat community, efforts were made to recycle gray water and use some alternative sewage treatment system. There were some who pumped waste into the bay, plus the perception of the public was that all the houseboat residents were pumping into the bay. When the building department suggested connecting to the sewer system in the 1950s, it was too expensive for the people living there. (Willoughby, 1959) Some of the original residents—either because they could not financially afford it or did not ethically believe it was necessary—presented other alternatives to hooking up to the sewer system. Sim Van Der Ryn, head of the State Office of Appropriate Technology, endorsed a compost toilet at a press conference at the *San Rafael* ferry. (Garlic Press, February 14, 1978)

The Richardson Bay Special Area Plan suggests another alternative, the honey barge:

"floating a large holding tank with pump-out mechanism (commonly called a honey barge) around to vessels used as residences. Under this system, sewage and gray water are pumped from the separate holding tanks into the larger barge holding tank for transport to shore side pump-out facility and sewage treatment system."

The plan admitted that there was little experience with such a system, and it would involve additional administration, maintenance, and regulation costs. The Regional Water Quality Control Board and Marin County Department of Environmental Health both "expressed skepticism about the economic feasibility and reliability of such a system."

When this issue ultimately became one that threatened the actual existence of the marinas, almost all complied and hooked up to the sewer system. In most marinas now, new houseboat berths have a direct connection to the local sewer system. By code, each houseboat has its own 30-40 gallon sewage and gray water receiving tank and ejector device that pump sewage and gray water into the sewer pipes that run underneath the piers and connect to the sewer system. Some marinas, like Galilee Harbor, have a "pump out" arrangement that is monitored by Sausalito. A plate is installed to prevent waste from being discharged overboard and the waste holding tanks are pumped out when full. (Sausalito City Council, 1990) Anchor-outs and live-aboards use pump-out facilities.

An anchor-out off Waldo Point. A 1977 article by Les Ledbetter in *The New York Times* quoted a "well-dressed resident of Sausalito" as saying "the hippies didn't die; they migrated from San Francisco across the Golden Gate to Gate 5 with all their filthy habits." (Ledbetter, March 14, 1977) This quote seemed to reflect the general feeling of most Sausalitans toward the houseboaters, even though a number of the boats (like the one shown here) were well maintained and had the means for recycling waste and water and generating power.

The lines for power, sewer, and water run beneath the marina piers at Kappas and Waldo Point.

The "pump out" connection is typically operated by connecting a hose to the waste tank in the boat. The waste is then pumped out and down the sewer lines under the dock into the sewer system on land.

In Galilee Harbor, a special arrangement with Sausalito allows water and power to run through hoses and cords from the docks, while sewage is discharged by pumping it out through a connection on the dock.

The water is shallower and calmer at this end of Richardson Bay, so lightweight foam was suitable flotation for a houseboat

## Floating Houses

By the early to mid-70s, development of Kappas Marina was nearing completion. Each pier was equipped with the required sewer, electrical, and water connections. To fill the open berths at Kappas Marina, various contractors began building houseboats for speculation. One builder, Ted Rose, worked with his partners and began building houseboats on one of the Marine Ways at Gate 3 in Sausalito. Beginning in 1971, Rose built about 28 houseboats on foam flotation. At that time, a 480 square foot houseboat on foam cost $2250 and the slip in Kappas cost $25/month. The designs for these houseboats were simple and compact, built on lightweight pieces of foam.

One of two similar houseboats on Kappas East Dock. Around this time the term "floating home" became popular.

A variety of small lightweight houseboats. Their age and size suggest that they were originally built on foam; today most have been transferred to concrete barges.

These homes were built on 3' thick blocks of 4' x 8' polystyrene foam, laid flat to create a 12' x 40' rectangle. The blocks were secured together with pressure treated wood and wood floor framing. The exterior walls were built like shear walls, and one or two shear walls were built across the middle. The "heavier rooms," like the kitchen and bathroom, with appliances, bathtub, sinks, and storage, were placed in the middle of the rectangle. This type of home weighed about 12,000 pounds and would sink the foam halfway. Builders soon realized that the position of the bathtub could tip and sink a boat and owners realized that it was important not to over furnish the home. (Rose, pers. comm.)

The *Compass Rose*, a houseboat built during the 1970s.

The *Compass Rose* has a picturesque setting on Issaquah Dock.

*Compass Rose.*
The living area.

*Compass Rose.* The dining nook.

*Compass Rose.*
The kitchen
area.

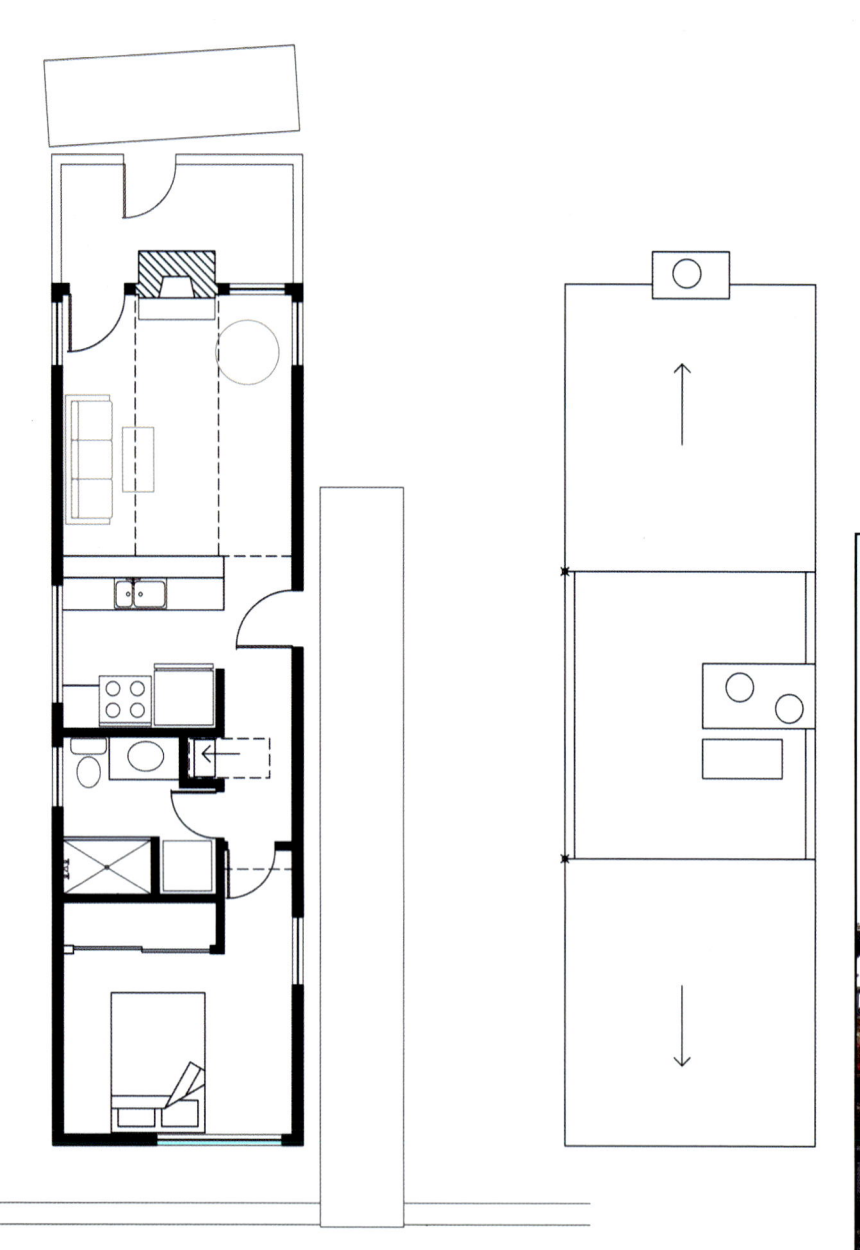

The plan of the *Compass Rose*, a 12' x 40' home on Styrofoam.

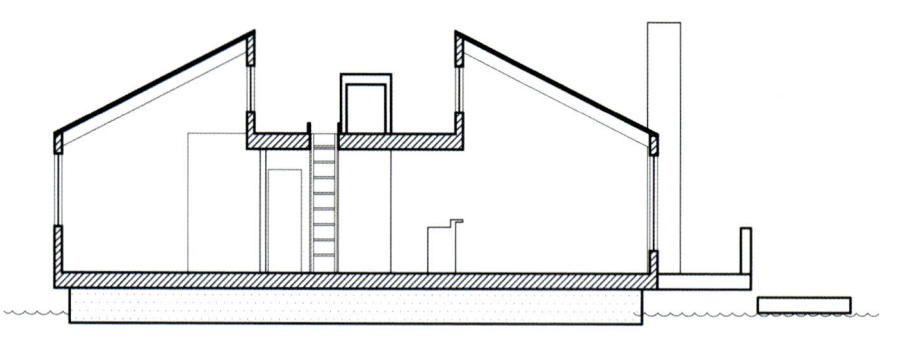

This roof detail was not uncommon in the houseboats. It brought more light into the boat and provided an area for a roof deck.

A sister boat to the *Compass Rose*, with a reversal of the angled roof.

Another houseboat of the same basic design as *Compass Rose*. Ted Rose, who built many houseboats of this style, recalls laying down sixteen blocks of foam to make a 16' x 32' rectangle, squaring it, then building up from there.

*A Compass Rose sister boat on Issaquah Dock.*

Rose recalls going to the Sausalito Building Department to get permits for the houseboats he was building at Gate 3. When they found out the boats were going to be located at Kappas and Waldo Point (Marin County), however, they did not want to be involved. When Marin County found out the boats were being built in Sausalito they did not want to be involved. Rose estimates he built 48-50 houseboats without permits for this reason. Other contractors probably encountered the same permitting dilemma. As shown in one County of Marin Department of Public Works Floating Home Inspection Report from 1975, it appears that during the 1970s Marin County was concerned with the residents having "occupancy permits," with inspection reports documenting deficiencies in existing construction rather than regulating new construction.

A small, lightweight, single story houseboat, less than 400 square feet.

A houseboat on what appears to still be foam.

160

A Kappas East Dock houseboat. Typically built on foam, many of the houseboats were built multiple times, mirroring the plan or changing little details.

This houseboat is the mirror image of the brown Kappas East houseboat, with some additions and alterations made—probably since its original construction.

Early aerial photos show *Luna di Miele* dating from the early 1970s; assessor records put its construction date at 1966. This houseboat is built with two bedroom/bath areas, each with a separate entrance, plus a common dining/living area. As noted, many of these boats were originally built on Styrofoam, then transferred to a concrete barge when they became available.

*Luna di Miele* has picturesque views of Waldo Point Harbor.

*Luna di Miele*, a floating home built in 1966, originally constructed on foam.

*Luna di Miele*. The living area with Main Dock beyond.

162

*Luna di Miele.* A hatch and folding ladder lead down to a 5' tall crawl space. The boat was originally built on another type of flotation, probably Styrofoam, then transferred to a concrete barge later.

*Luna di Miele.* A unique built in bench and storage over the vaulted living room. The view out the window at high tide is of the San Francisco skyline.

According to one well-documented chronology published in *The Garlic Press* (2-14-78), 1977 was a year of change for the houseboat community at Waldo Point. Seeing the construction of Kappas' expensive, suburban style houseboat marina, the residents at Waldo Point formed the Waldo Point Association (WPA) to work with the developers of Waldo Point Harbor. WPA sought to create an area of low-income housing where the less affluent members of the houseboat community could moor their houseboats as they had done in the past. But development continued, not without resistance from the community, and eventually the creek that served the area was filled in and the Marine Dock, A Dock, began construction August 9, 1977. Less than a month later, Spreckels House was demolished, followed by the construction of B Dock (today known as Issaquah Dock) The demise of the community at Waldo Point and its replacement with an affluent houseboat marina development was imminent, and with the demise of the existing community came the start of extinction for their style of architecture.

The marine dock was the first dock built at Waldo Point Harbor. Today, it is still the location of Nelson Marine, the pile driver, and the structural engineer who still designs concrete basement barges.

163

The entrance for "A" Dock or the "Marine Dock."

**The Garlic Press**

In 1975, when Kappas was completing his houseboat marina, the residents were incited to organize in order to prevent such a suburbanized houseboat community, and began publishing *The Garlic Press*, a local newspaper covering current events at the Harbor. One Waldo Point survey in 1977 recognized that there were five "neighborhoods" at Waldo Point, with a total of 203 households. The survey indicated that most people there made less than $10,000 annually, but about 20% made over $10,000 annually. The majority of people were between 18 and 39, and 15% of the community was children. Each household averaged one car.

Issaquah Dock was followed by the construction of Liberty Dock. Of all the houseboat docks built in Richardson Bay, these two—shaped like two hands encompassing a large sailing basin—were thought to be the most desirable. The berths toward the end had deep water and afforded incredible views of Richardson Bay plus San Francisco and Mount Tamalpais beyond. Wealthy individuals who could afford the berthage came in and leased berths, then commissioned houseboats to be built. It is said that on Issaquah Dock, where tenants of higher notoriety berthed, only select tenants from the original community were asked to berth, and the majority of houseboats were of a newer, more expensive style—larger and built on concrete barges.

Issaquah Dock forms the left (or north) side and Liberty Dock forms the right (or south side), encompassing a large open basin. Main Dock, original to the turn-of-the-century shipyard, and the arks hug the shore.

164

The entrance to B Dock, known as Issaquah Dock.

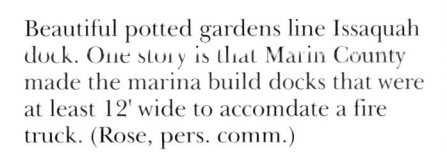

Beautiful potted gardens line Issaquah dock. One story is that Marin County made the marina build docks that were at least 12' wide to accomdate a fire truck. (Rose, pers. comm.)

**Piers vs. Planks In The Mud**

The construction of piers with piles and gangways to access each houseboat was contrary to the original community, where boats were accessed by boards laid in the mud and by stepping from boat to boat. One tenant recalls seeing electrical wiring strung through floating Gallo wine bottles. (Earhart, pers. comm.) Though this informal, yet quite personal, form of working with neighbors was lost with the construction of the docks, a more formal, but still inviting type of access to the boats evolved. Today many of the docks, especially Issaquah Dock, are bordered by elaborate gardens, each maintained by the individual houseboat tenants.

## Introduction of the Concrete Barge

A *New York Times* article of January 23, 1969, by Muarry Davis, "lauded" ferro-cement houseboats as strong and safe and noted that boat builder SeaFerro of Fort Lauderdale had begun designing cement houseboats. The first cement boat, according to the article, was built in 1855 by Jean Louis Lambot. The material was seriously developed in the U.S. in the 1950s. With some imagination, the form evolved from a boat hull, or barge, to a full height "basement" that was below the water. Forbes Kiddoo brought this idea to the houseboat community and it evolved from there.

Investors in the marina, their friends, and their associates were all ready to build their houseboat when they saw the marina was going to be constructed. The concrete barge provided an opportunity to build a bigger more luxurious houseboat. This houseboat was known as the Wesley Oyama *Wildflower Barge*. The concrete hull, shell, and first two floors were built by Forbes Kiddoo. Craftsmen were flown in from Japan to finish the third level. Oyama was one of the investors in the marina, and, the story goes, was one of the five families permitted to trade with the US after World War II. (Rose, pers. comm.)

*Wildflower Barge.*
A window detail.

*Wildflower Barge.*
The entrance.

When the marina and houseboat community became legal, banks loaned money against the houseboats and insurance companies typically provided insurance. Houseboats suddenly had value and more money was being invested in the construction of the buildings. Wood and steel did not prove to be long term solutions for creating a barge to float a house, so engineers like Ed Beattie and builders like Forbes Kiddoo refined the idea of a concrete barge designed to support the house or boat. This created a "basement" and maximized the space allowed by the new building code, was more watertight, and required less maintenance than a traditional boat. It was constructed much like a house with a basement, except for the fact that it sat in water rather than soil.

At extreme low tide, one can see the construction of the entire concrete basement barge. It is built like a typical foundation, except that it sits in water rather than dirt. This appears to be a Kiddoo barge based on the flared edge at the top of the concrete walls.

At the time of this writing, there appears to be only one primary concrete barge builder in the Bay area. According to the stamp on the side of this new barge, it is Ian Moody's (Aquamaison Inc.) 338th barge.

A concrete barge waiting for the tide.

The concrete barge is constructed like a basement, then floated out into Richardson Bay to an area that is the correct water depth. One technique for transferring an old boat to a barge is to sink the barge, then float the old houseboat over it. As the tide falls, the old houseboat settles onto the barge with careful leveling and coordination. The water in the basement is pumped out, and when the tide rises again the home floats.

The concrete barge increased the size of houseboats well beyond what could be supported by foam.

168

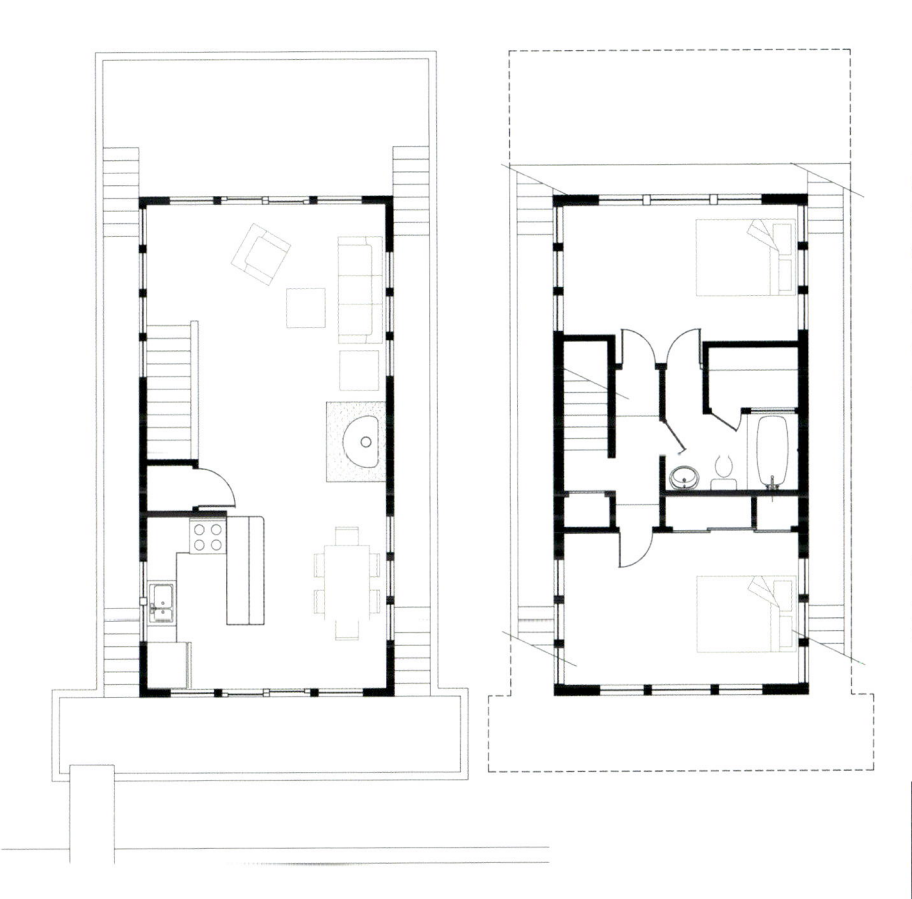

By the 1980s, building a house on a concrete basement was the primary, if not the only, way to build a houseboat. The term "houseboat" was used less, and replaced almost exclusively with the term "floating home" in the houseboat marinas. In the Marin County Code, for instance, almost all references to "houseboat" have been replaced with "floating home." In some reports, the term is used as an all inclusive one covering any residence that floats. Today, there are only a few houses floating on the original boat flotation left in the marinas. Houseboats are still anchored in Richardson Bay however, many of them dating from the early 1960s.

A Kiddoo houseboat, 17' x 32' *Baan Phra Thong*, has a simple, intricately detailed plan, designed for a concrete barge basement.

*Baan Phra Thong* has one of the most desirable slips on Issaquah Dock.

169

*Baan Phra Thong.* A two-foot wide ledge around the perimeter of the barge strengthens it and provides access to all sides of the houseboat for maintenance. Other residents also point out that it gives the boat more of a floating appearance, one of "hovering over the water."

The artwork of *Baan Phra Thong*.

*Baan Phra Thong* interior. Note the ladder in the ceiling, which folds down to access a skylight leading to a roof deck.

170

*Baan Phra Thong*. The kitchen.

*Baan Phra Thong*. Many of the homes have a stacking washer and dryer hidden in a closet.

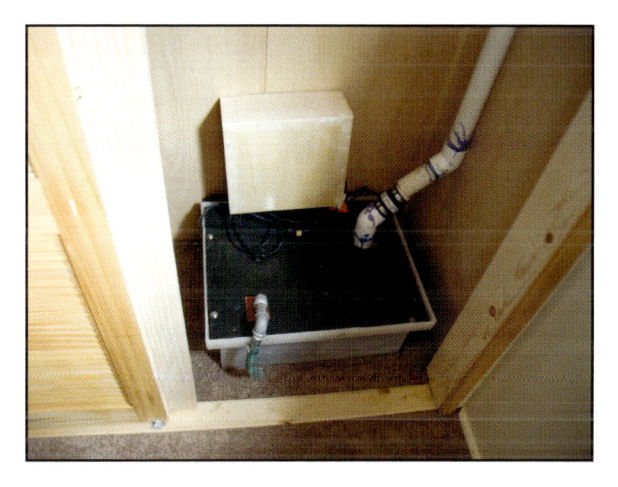

*Baan Phra Thong*. Each houseboat must have a holding tank, and all drains in the houseboat lead to this tank. A flexible connection on the exterior connects it to the sewage lines under the pier, and these connect to the county sewer system. This tank is hidden inside a closet.

*Baan Phra Thong*. An arched gangway that rises and falls with the tide leads to the home.

*Baan Phra Thong*. A wood lined sauna is found on the lower level. A glass window separates the sauna from the bathroom.

171

## A Civil War

By the time Liberty Dock was built, it was obvious that the community was becoming divided, and the people who wanted to be legal and have a berth took the opportunity to stay on Liberty Dock. Many of the creative, well-maintained original houseboats berthed there; today many have been added onto and enlarged from their original forms. More houses were built by speculative builders, many of them following the same design.

A small houseboat on Liberty Dock dwarfed between two large ones.

One of the large houseboats on Liberty Dock with a premium end slip.

Another large Liberty Dock houseboat.

172

One of the older Liberty Dock houseboats.

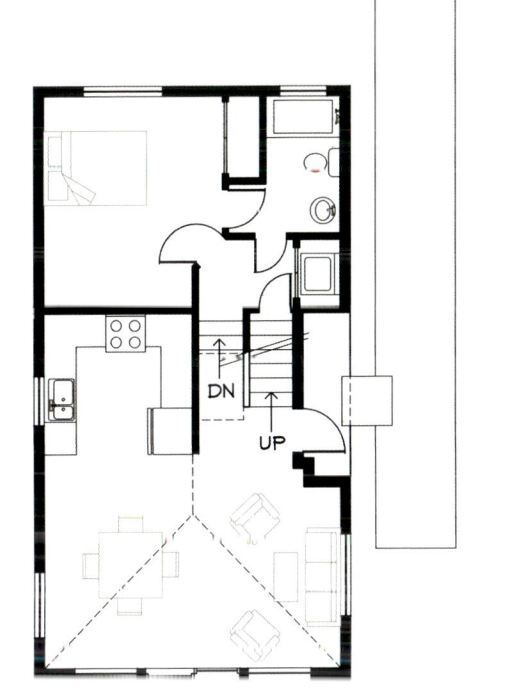

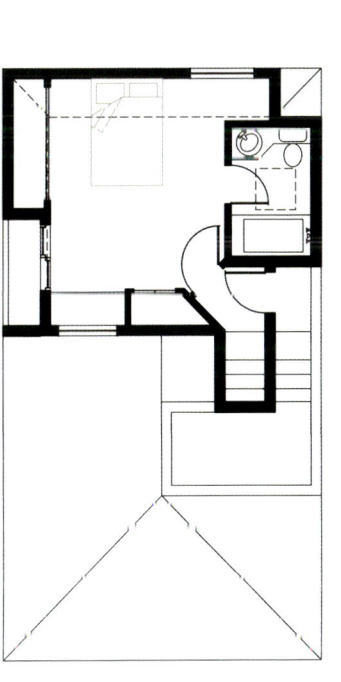

*Iwok*, A 20' x 36' split level floating home by Ian Moody built in the 1980s.

173

### The "Houseboat Wars"

At the time the population boomed and drugs became more prevalent at Waldo Point, those who had moved there in the early 1960s were typically in their thirties with kids. They had grown accustomed to the waterfront lifestyle and wanted to stay. One group, who believed there should be affordable housing on the water, moved to the waterfront inside the Sausalito city limits where requirements were more lax. Another group stayed at Waldo Point and supported the development of the harbor into a legal houseboat marina. Although the hook up to sewage was expensive, they could see the practicality if insured a berth for the long term. (Berdahl, Part 1, 1972) Yet another group decided to stay at Waldo Point and fight the development. As construction proceeded, eviction notices were issued and arrests were made, as this group protested what they perceived to be the destruction of their community. One group even filed a suit to protect the ferryboats. In their 1978 Valentine's Day issue, *The Garlic Press* laid out a chronology documenting all of the actions, arrests, evictions, and other events that show the general flavor of the turbulent times as the community watched the Waldo Point Harbor developers essentially demolish their buildings…and their community. This era was known as "The Houseboat Wars" and the general atmosphere is documented in a film called *The Last Free Ride* by Ray Nolan and Sal Rouda. Others, though, were ready for development and called this time a "Civil War." (Earhart, pers. comm.)

*Stonesoup*, on Liberty Dock, was hand built by Marilyn Earhart and her husband in Benecia in 1969. Named after the fairy tale "Stone soup," it had bits and pieces from all over, including parts salvaged from the Western Addition, "six copper clad windows from Cleveland Wrecking," and a turned post from Gilroy. The design, before the addition on the lower left, reflected the California water tower design: a square box on top of a round cylinder. The boat has since been moved to a barge and passed on to a relative. The owners, who lived on *Stonesoup* for fourteen years, went on to build *Vichychoisse*. (Earhart, pers. comm.)

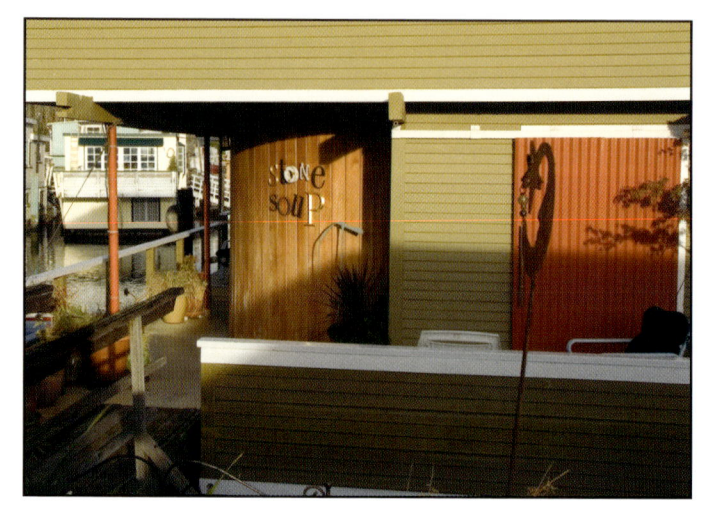

*Stonesoup*.

*Vichychoisse* was the second houseboat for this family at Waldo Point. This photo describes the open feel in the interior of *Vichychoisse*.

*Vichychoisse*. Glasses and spoons create an artistic display.

*Vichychoisse's* exterior is unpretenious.

*Vichychoisse*. A sun porch.

175

A view of Clipper Yacht Harbor from *Vichychoisse*. At high tide, you can see the highrises in SanFrancisco.

A porthole from a ship serves as a window in *Vichychoisse*.

In this old aerial photo from the Waldo Point Harbor office, Waldo Point Harbor is nearing completion. Houseboats are still tied together with homemade docks between the new piers. *Courtesy Ted Rose.*

176

Main Dock, a short dock in between Issaquah and Liberty, was the original dock at Waldo Point left over from the days when the shipyard was there. Many of the original houseboats, some rumored to be original from the early shipyard days, stayed there and more speculative houseboats were built on foam and concrete barges.

A 1982 houseboat on Main Dock.

An ark on Main Dock. Many of the arks on or near Main Dock, though renovated numerous times, are original to the Arques Marina and many of the houseboats are the oldest in the community.

A houseboat built during construction of the marina, dating to 1975 according to assessor records.

This houseboat from the late 1960s, shown here are an extreme low tide, was originally berthed in what is now Kappas Yacht Harbor. Before Kappas Houseboat Harbor was built, George Kappas allowed all kinds of boats in the yacht harbor. This resident remembers it as an authentic "live-work" environment: fishing boats alongside houseboats alongside pleasure boats. When the houseboat harbor was built, Kappas offered the residents a slip in the new harbor but many did not accept because the water was too shallow. This houseboat moved to Main Dock, where space was available. The lower level has a complete gym, and the dark interior, low ceilings, and detailing inside create a 1960s atmosphere.

Originally built as a quonset hut on an LCVP, this houseboat on Main Dock appears in early photos of the marina.

Said to be one of the original arks in Arques Shipyard, now floating on what appears to be a Kiddoo style barge.

By the time South Forty Dock (the dock closest to the Sausalito city limits line) was built, there was still a group of houseboaters resisting the development and regulation, and some resisting the high berthage and requirements to upgrade systems on their houseboats to connect to the docks. Some were simply resisting the conventional development of straight docks with massive houseboats dwarfing smaller ones. In the end, the houseboaters and developers reached a plan they agreed on for South Forty Dock—one that reflected more of the original pre-development community and afforded the small boats light and views amongst the larger houseboats. This dock is where many of the original houseboats that were saved from redevelopment now reside.

South Forty Dock, just a few feet from the city limits of Sausalito, is set apart from the other docks when approached by land.

South Forty Dock, with Mount Tamalpias beyond.

South Forty Dock with the hills of Sausalito and the Marin Headlands beyond.

A view from South Forty Dock.

Unlike the other docks, South Forty Dock has what the residents call "pods" off the main dock that typically three boats tie to. The "pod" becomes a front yard for the three neighbors and gives the smaller boats better light and views.

A 1970s houseboat, less than 1000 square feet, according to assessor records.

Many of the pods are decorated with seating and artwork for the three neighbors.

This brought a new type of construction retrofitting the older boats: putting the boats on concrete barges. This was probably the least expensive way for owners of these self-made houseboats to improve the perception of "safety," in terms of flotation. There is some question as to whether these boats were pressured by Marin County, the marina, insurance companies, or banks (now part of the equation since the houseboats had value) to move to a barge, rather than maintaining the hull as one would a boat. This could be possible, as Marin County's Floating Home Inspection checklist from 1975 notes that if the inspector determined that a boat was "unstable" or "structurally inadequate," if the freeboard was less than 15" (a definite possibility in some of the LCVPs), or if any of ninety-two other requirements were not met, the houseboat could not be occupied. The list was vague and interpretation was left to the Marine Inspector. This was a change from the 1970 Marin County Application for Permit to Occupy, which, on paper, did not prohibit occupancy based on the type of structure, sewer system, or water supply.

A free form roof over a 1971 300 square foot single story houseboat on an LCVP hull.

Many boats were moved to concrete barges. Some cut away parts of the boat to help eliminate moisture problems.

181

A houseboat transferred to a barge.

A "cottage houseboat" on South Forty Dock, originally on an LCVP hull.

Cottage houseboat interior.

Cottage houseboat. The master bedroom overlooks the living room.

Cottage houseboat kitchen. Most of the interior is finished in wood.

Cottage houseboat. The master bedroom with a variety of windows.

Cottage houseboat on a LCVP hull. A simple plan, but an intricate three dimensional puzzle with shapes intersecting as shown in the interior photos.

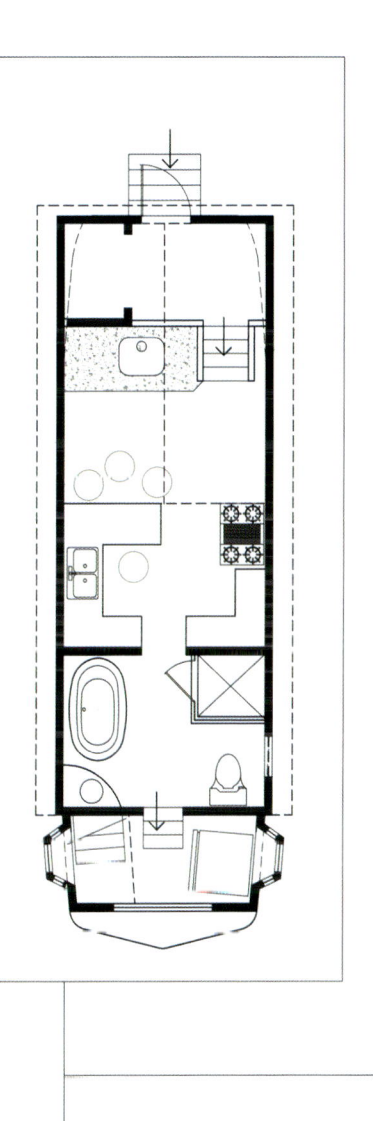

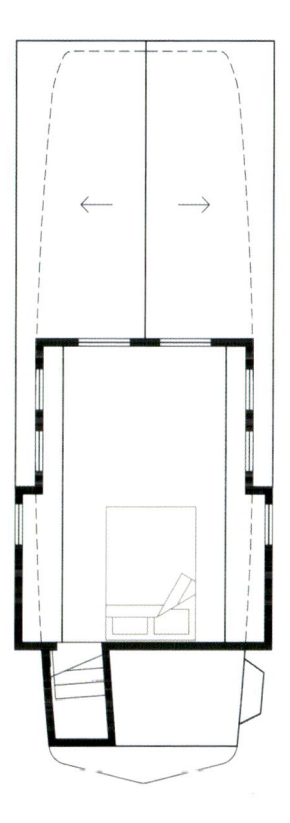

185

## Whimsical Architecture

"Whimsy" seems to be a common thread throughout the various periods of houseboat development, but seems to have become more pronounced once Kappas and Waldo Point Harbor marinas were built and people had assigned berths. The idea of making a house out of a train car or boat was something of a novelty. Sexton, in his book *Cottages*, says these boats were most likely built "out of infatuation" rather than necessity. (Sexton, 1989) But, even though the new residents could afford any kind of design or construction, it is interesting that many chose to reflect the community's original intent: reusing materials that would otherwise be thrown away.

The *Train Wreck* was a train car converted to living space and integrated into a houseboat.

Comparing photos with a Marin Independent article by John Moses July 13, 1996, this could have been the *Mt. Eden*. The *Mt. Eden* was a replica of a sternwheeler riverboat, except that it ran on diesel. It was the "dream yacht of Harlen Soeten...founder of the San Francisco Maritime museum." It is berthed today in Sausalito Marineways Harbor.

This houseboat was made from a caboose in the late 1970s by Edmund Davis. (Sexton, 1989) By that time, most of the artists were adapting recycled materials out of a creative urge rather than necessity. Houseboat construction immediately after development of the harbor seemed to reflect the original intention of the community: reusing materials that would otherwise be thrown away.

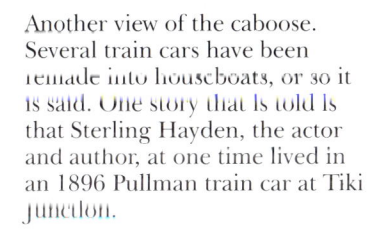

Another view of the caboose. Several train cars have been remade into houseboats, or so it is said. One story that is told is that Sterling Hayden, the actor and author, at one time lived in an 1896 Pullman train car at Tiki Junction.

187

Also, perhaps more recently, there has been a move toward using colors and materials that are traditionally not accepted in neighborhoods on land. Houseboats that show up as natural wood, grey, and white in the early days of the community have been changed to bright colors of red, yellow, and purple, creating a kind of "Disneyland" atmosphere. Residents also display a variety of styles and interpretations of art, and exotic plants line the docks. One thought is that even though the new Marin County code has created a "shoebox" houseboat design, the residents are still inspired to express their individuality using color and art. (Moss, pers. comm.)

This houseboat built by Rodger March in the 1980s, originally with naturally finished wood siding, now uses a bright, weather resistant metal siding in a color scheme not typically found in land residences.

A small, one story purple houseboat.

A purple houseboat with magenta trim.

Pink, purple, and aquamarine houseboats.

Colorful entry with blue door in Galilee Harbor.

A log cabin houseboat.

## Affordable Architecture

In 1977, when the community still had hopes for continued existence, several proposals were discussed with developers and authorities to construct a "Gate 6 ghetto" behind the *Charles Van Damme* ferry. This concept of creating affordable waterfront housing for some of the houseboaters carried into Sausalito, when some of these residents moved to the Napa Street Pier and later created the Galilee Cooperative. Some of these boats were original to the community, but many have been replaced with other forms of affordable houseboats.

An affordable houseboat in Galilee Harbor.

A boat as an affordable home.

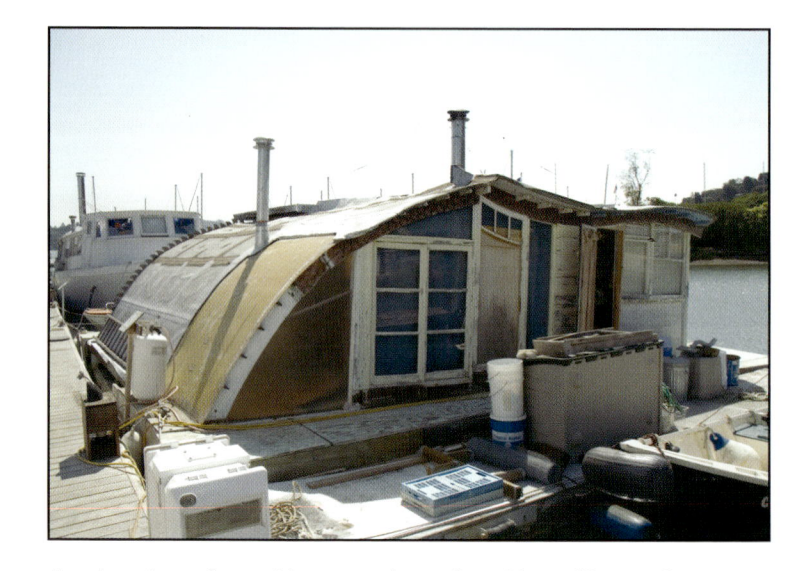

A unique houseboat with a curved metal roof in Galilee Harbor.

Another houseboat in Galilee Harbor. It is said that many of the houseboats in Galilee moved to that location when they could not get a slip at Waldo Point Harbor.

Another group of houseboats created the Gates Cooperative (aka "Gates Coop" or "Gate 6" to some) at Waldo Point. This group of boats exists between Main and Issaquah dock and, like Galilee, contains some of the initial flavor of the original community. Many people believe that these were the people that were shut out from obtaining a berth in the marina. Perhaps they resisted conformance a little too long, were not reliable in paying their rent, did not have the money, or did not have the money at the right time, but while they were unable to obtain slips at the docks, they continued to stay.

The mural at the entrance to Gates Coop.

An overview of Gates Coop from the water.

Wiring in Gates Coop. As the tide rises and falls, the wires tighten and loosen.

Houseboat with peace sign in Gates Coop.

According to a Marin County Community Development Agency memo on February 21, 2006, when houseboats like these get a slip in Waldo Point Harbor, they will need to be placed on a concrete barge. In some cases, Styrofoam may be used.

Another view of Gates Coop.

**Gates Cooperative Fill Project**

Gates Coop is still trying to acquire legal status for their community, much like Arques did for Waldo Point Harbor in the late 1960s, early '70s. From 1993 to 1995, Gates Cooperative, in an elaborate effort to settle litigation between the State of California, Waldo Point Harbor, Gates Cooperative, and the County of Marin, conducted a fill reduction project at Waldo Point Harbor. This project primarily destroyed, but also relocated, 24 houseboats in order to obtain approval of an additional 41 berths at Waldo Point Harbor. Family photos document the boats' existence and others show the boats' destruction or move via trailer. Sometime in the near future, these 41 berths will be worked into the harbor and the old boats will be replaced with new. (Bradley, pers. comm.) (Koestel, 1995)

In 2006, now legally defined as a "live-aboard low-income community," Gates Cooperative is still struggling to have legal berths in the harbor. In the meantime, under the funding of a Marin County Community Development Agency Block Grant (CDBG) they are "rehabilitating" the boats by putting them on concrete barges. In a CDBG memo of February 21, 2006 recommending allocation of funds, the staff recognizes that Styrofoam may be substituted for concrete as a more affordable solution.

## The Last Houseboats, The Anchor-Outs

As noted earlier, there was a big push to remove and demolish boats anchored in Richardson Bay. Many people moved on, but a few stayed. Existing as an anchor-out is a difficult life. Residents must produce their own power, typically with wind or sun. Water, groceries, propane, laundry—everything must be hauled to and from shore with a dinghy. Many boats have their own composting system and grey water recycle system to discharge of waste. The boat is not protected as it is in a marina, so maintenance is a constant process.

Anchor-outs still exist today. In the late 1980s, however, there was a movement to clean up Richardson Bay and remove the anchored out boats. The boats that Marin County determines are "illegal" are brought to the Corps of Engineers dock and destroyed. At times, entire boats are on the "pile."

During the abatement of houseboats at Gate 6 (aka Gates Coop) Waldo Point Harbor, specific houseboats were called out for destruction. (Koestel, 1995) *Courtesy of Ted Rose.*

For an anchor-out, a dingy is a necessity. It becomes a car on the water.

Solar panels provide some of the power for this anchor-out houseboat.

A lifeboat converted to an anchored-out houseboat, with the multi-million dollar houses of Strawberry and Tiburon beyond. Note the wind generator on the port side of the boat, used to create power.

An anchor-out with a dinghy tied up at his front door.

**A Floating Island**

One anchor-out, Forbes Kiddoo, built one of the most opulent, imaginative homes in the area—so big that it is called a floating island. Kiddoo describes it as having 40 tons of topsoil, 100 tons of sand, 120 tons or rock and 18 palm trees. (Kiddoo, pers. comm.) When people talk of Forbes' Island the stories are fantastic: an organ in every room, several bars, underwater submarine airlocks…"the world of a wanna-be Captain Nemo." A *New York Times* article references guests who talked of three-day parties and black tie events of Bach and Mozart. The island is huge, with an estimated weight of 400 tons, 15 rooms, a wine cellar, a treatment plant for sewage, portholes, a lighthouse, a gazebo, a beach, and palm trees to date. (Cummings, July 3, 1982) In spite of Kiddoo's popularity, his unique lifestyle off of Sausalito in Richardson Bay came to an end when government agencies decided to get rid of the anchor-outs in Richardson Bay in the late 1980s and he was forced to move the island to another location.

Another anchored-out houseboat with solar panels on the deck and a wind generator on the bow.

A boat anchored out.

An anchor-out with the houseboats of Waldo Point Harbor behind.

An anchor-out on a foggy day.

# Chapter 6
# The Future

By 1985, it was recognized that most of the artists, writers, and craftsmen who were the principal occupants of houseboats in the 1950s, '60s, and '70s had been replaced with more affluent residents who could afford the high berthing fees of the new marinas and the escalating construction costs. The appearance of the houseboat community had changed. In many cases, boxy shaped structures replaced the imaginatively designed boats. (BCDC, 1985, p. 7)

One original resident had no idea that the houseboat harbors at Waldo Point and Kappas would become so expensive and stylish once they were legalized. Today, many original residents miss the early lifestyle that shaped the community, but admit that similar developments have occurred in other artists' communities and the shift from an artists' community to an affluent one was "inevitable." (Beattie, pers. comm.)

Most people today choose to live on a houseboat because they want to be closer to nature, but the community and safety of the docks are additional attractions. At one time, a large percentage of the population consisted of divorced, widowed, or retired women. Today, many houseboats are second homes, with dock neighbors seen as built in security when the owner is away at other locations.

> **A Place to Retire**
>
> After retiring, a former mayor of Sausalito moved to the houseboat community in order to take advantage of the safety of the community and a smaller place to maintain. A friend, whose husband had recently passed away, visited her there and decided to sell her house in Castro Valley and move to Issaquah Dock. Later, the friend's daughter, who lives on the East Coast, bought a houseboat to rent out, while the friend's son bought one on another dock to live in. Recently, another friend purchased the ark next door to retire to.

Today, in 2006, houseboat prices range from $250,000 (for a "teardown") to more than $1 million. One story claims that a 1700 square foot houseboat in 2006 sells for $949,000, and in 2005 prices went up 18%. (Liam Mayclem, Eye on the Bay, 11-28-05) Mortgages have shorter terms and higher interest rates, there is only one primary company that will insure houseboats, and slip fees range between $500 and $1200 a month. In Waldo Point Harbor, each tenant has a ten year lease with an option for an additional ten years. With regard to construction, there is currently only one contractor in Sausalito with a reputation for building houseboat barges. These added together make houseboat construction and purchase very expensive—and hard to justify financially for the average upper or middle class family. But the attraction of the natural setting convinces some people, typically wealthier ones, to buy there.

Escalating property values are encouraging houseboat owners to enlarge and improve their homes and maximize square footage. In order to do this, one stretches to the limits of what the building code will allow. Most everyone in today's houseboat communities in Marin County agrees that the "pre-code houseboats are much more creative than the code compliant shoeboxes they are building today." (Sennett, pers. comm.) Although some would like to keep one of the older houseboats, some need to be renovated extensively. To do so would mean complying with code, and many of the older houseboats do not comply. In such cases, it is more lucrative financially to destroy the boat and build a newer, larger one.

It has also become a tricky exercise for the government agencies to maintain an appropriate balance between what is environmentally appropriate and what is appropriate for the property owners and tenants.

A new houseboat under construction in 2006. Many residents believe that this design evolved out of the Marin County Codes and the need for the new owners or speculative builders to maximize square footage. The energy code, updated in 2005, is a balance of a number of requirements, but in the end typically reduces the amount of glazing significantly.

Detail of the houseboat under construction.

This 1950s era, 320 square foot houseboat on an LCVP hull sold for $190,000 in early 2006. The realtor sold the houseboat as a "tear down," inferring that the owner was selling the rights to the 12' x 42' foot slip and the buyer would replace it with a home that maximized square footage.

A new houseboat under construction on Main Dock. The design reflects the old energy code, and uses the maximum glazing possible at that time. Some builders believe that the new energy code has influenced the design of houseboats both in the use of alternative materials and minimizing glazing.

A new houseboat under construction in Gates Coop.

A houseboat on the way to a slip off of Kappas Houseboat Harbor.

Some residents are concerned that some of the more historic houseboats will not be preserved and will end up like the *Charles Van Damme*.

**Balancing Fill and Wildlife**

In the past few years, in an effort to further meet the objective of removing fill in the bay, BCDC has been removing the log rafts around the marinas. Ironically, this has an effect of eliminating the high tide refuge for shorebirds (forcing them to migrate to areas other than Richardson Bay) as well as eliminating a roosting area for diving birds including cormorants and terns. (1-24-06 letter to Katarina Galacados, Army Corps of Engineers, from Barbara Salzman and letter To Robert Hickman, BCDC, 2-23-88 by Barbara Salzman, Chair) With this roosting area eliminated, and the development of upland tide areas, it is likely that many of these wild birds may migrate to other areas than Richardson Bay.

A circa 2004 photo showing one of the log rafts used by shorebirds that has been removed from Richardson Bay. *Courtesy Pat Lawrence.*

Legally, Waldo Point Harbor is under threat of reconfiguration since it never complied with the original BCDC permit. Kappas Houseboat Marina is still trying to renew its permit that expired in 1992. Some of its houseboat slips are over Marin County's underwater streets and while BCDC approved it in 1972, this item is a point of contention in the renewal. Perhaps due to frustration at the local government level, a solution to the issue was written into legislation by State Senator Carole Migden, bill SB1701. If approved by the governor, Steckler Pacific, the owners of Kappas Houseboat Marina, will trade some of its underwater land for the underwater streets the houseboats float over. (Speich, 2006)

In addition, the anchor-outs are not legal. There are still approximately 90 vessels, 40 of those used as residences, that still anchor off of Waldo Point and the Sausalito waterfront. One lifeboat has been there as a residence since the mid-1960s. (Bang, pers. comm.)

The permanently anchored-out houseboats are still considered to be "squatting" on public land.

On the Sausalito waterfront, the number of houseboats today is minimal compared to what it once had been, and the possibility of a large houseboat marina like those at the north end of Richardson Bay is small. However, the possibility exists that the opposite may happen. The Sausalito government has viewed some waterfront dwellers as low-income and in need of affordable housing, like the houseboats from the 1960s. It is possible that some of their waterfront marinas, like Galilee, may serve to meet Sausalito's affordable housing state required quota. (Sausalito City official, pers. comm.) However, according to all the regulations currently in place, there will be no new houseboat communities on the bay and the existing communities will have to re-establish their existence periodically to BCDC, to ensure that they still serve the interest of the people of California.

The anchor-outs off of the Sausalito waterfront, both transient and long term.

Development plans for the Sausalito Marineways property, where this houseboat is berthed, are currently under review

Very little change is expected in regards to the existing houseboats in the established marinas off of the Sausalito waterfront.

# Bibliography

Barr, Barbara, and Barbara Turner Sachs. *The Artists' & Writers' Cookbook*. Sausalito, CA: Angel Island Publications, Inc., 1961.

Bay Conservation and Development Commission (BCDC). "Houseboats and Liveaboard Boats." Open-file report, July 1985.

Bay Area Census online, "1980 Census," http://www.bayareacensus.ca.gov/cities/Sausalito70.htm (accessed November 13, 2006).

Berdahl, Doris. "Herb Madden – Land Owner and Developer." *Marin Scope* (CA), week of December 14-20, 1971.

Berdahl, Doris. "Waldo Point – Can It Survive A Clean Up? Part 3." *Marin Scope* (CA), week of May 30-June 5, 1972.

Berdahl, Doris. "Waldo Point – Can It Survive A Clean Up? Part 1." *Marin Scope* (CA), week of April 25-May 2, 1972.

Berdahl, Doris. "Waldo Point – Can It Survive A Clean Up? Part 2." *Marin Scope* (CA), week of May 16-22, 1972.

Berdahl, Doris. "Houseboats – Do They Have A Future On The Sausalito Waterfront?" *Marin Scope* (CA), week of April 25-May 2, 1972.

Berkeley in the Sixties Production Partnership. *Berkeley in the Sixties*. DVD. CA: Kitchell Films in Association with P.O.V. Theatrical Films, 1990.

CA State Military Department., The CA State Military Museum. "Historic California Posts, Stations and Airfields Naval Net Depot, Tiburon (Naval Coaling Station, California City)." Working paper, http://www.militarymuseum.org/Tiburon.html

Cummings, Judith. "To Marin County, No Houseboater is an Island." *New York Times*, July 3, 1982.

Earth Mechanics Inc. "Waterfront Residential Use Study." Open-file report, December 1983, 2-2, 5-8.

Dennis, Ben, and Betsy Case. *Houseboat*. Seattle: Smuggler's Cove Publishing, 1977.

DKS Associates. *Sausalito Transportation/Circulation Study*. Open-file documentation, October 1983.

Dubin, Beverly. *Water Squatters*. Santa Barbara: Capra Press, 1975.

Gabor, Mark. *Houseboats: Living on Water*. New York: Ballantine Books, 1979.

Frank, Phil. "There Were Houseboats Before Supervisors." *Garlic Press*, March 1977.

Gimler, Christine. "Staff Report to the Planning Commission." Marin County Community Development Agency, March 14, 2005, p. 2-3.

Hayton-Keeva, S. *Jaunita!: The madcap adventures of a legendary restaurateur*. Vineburg, CA: Sagn Books, 1990, 107-130.

Hill, Otis. "Russell Grisham and the 'Drydocks.'" *Marin Scope* (CA), October 12-18, 1971.

Hillson, Major Franklin J. "Barrage balloons for low-level air defense." *Airpower Journal*, Summer 1989, http://www.airpower.maxwell.af.mil/airchronicles/apj/apj89/hillson.html

Hoffman, George. *Saucelito-$au$alito*. Corte Madera, CA: A Woodward Book, 1976.

Issaquah Historical Society, "Issaquah Ferry Chronology." Working paper, 2006, http://www.issaquahhistory.org/sites/ferry_chron.htm

Koestel, Jane. "WPH Gates Cooperative Fill Reduction Project 1993-1995." Open-file documentation, Gates Cooperative, May 1, 1995

Ledbetter, Les. "Redevelopment Could End 'Free Ride' in Houseboats." *New York Times*, March 14, 1977.

Marin County California. Marin County, CA County Code, Floating Home Adjustments and Deviations, Chapter 22.46. Marin County, CA, 2003.

Marin County California. Marin County, CA County Code, Floating Homes, Chapter 22.32.075, III-81. Marin County, CA, 2003.

Marin County California. Marin County, CA County Code, Regulation of the Construction and Maintenance of Floating Homes, Chapter 19.18. Marin County, CA, 2003.

Marin County California. Marin County, CA County Code, Compartmentation and Flotation, Chapter 19.18.340. Marin County, CA, 2003.

Marin County Community Development Agency, memo to Richardson Bay Local Area committee from Bateman, Ford and Thaler, Recommendations for Funding, February 21, 2006.

*Marin Scope* (CA). "Houseboats Ordered to Scrap Heap." May 25, 1971.

Marin-Independent Journal, "The Fabulous World of Don Arques." *Marin Magazine,* September 14, 1957, p. M2-M7.

*Marin-Independent Journal.* "Ark Dwellers Cherish Water Sky." July 18, 1959.

Moses, John. "Marin's Unique Real Estate." *Marin-Independent Journal.* July 15, 1996.

Nolan, Ray and S. Rouda. 1974. *Last Free Ride.* Sausalito, CA: Ray Nolan Films.

Peltenburg, Edgar, ed. *Early Society in Cyprus.* Edinburgh: Edinburgh University Press, 1989.

Pollard's Lessee v. Hagan et al., 3 Howard, 212 (1845). Quoted in M. Scott "The Future of San Francisco Bay" (Berkeley, CA: Institute of Governmental Studies, 1963), p. 2.

Public Laws of the U.S., 1st sess., 31st Cong., 1850 pp 452-453. Quoted in M. Scott "The Future of San Francisco Bay" (Berkeley, CA: Institute of Governmental Studies, 1963), p. 2.

Rudofsky, Bernard. *Architecture without Architects.* Hartford, CT: Connecticut Printers, Inc. for Museum of Modern Art, New York, 1964.

Sausalito California. Sausalito Municipal Code. (1995).

Sausalito California. Sausalito Municipal Code. (2003).

Sausalito City Council. Resolution No. 3979 Resolution Of The Sausalito City Council Upholding, And Modifying Planning Commission Resolution No. 1990 – 12 Making Ceqa Findings And Adopting Mitigation Measures And Granting Conditional Use Permits No. 88-147-A, -B, -C, -D For Property Known As Galilee Harbor, Base Of Anpa Street, And Approving Certain Related Encroachment Permit Request And Denying The Appeal Filed By Velma Gamble, Et Al. (Sausalito, 1990).

*Sausalito News* (CA). "Annexation Channel Job, Aim of Chamber of Commerce." November 22, 1945, p.1.

*Sausalito News* (CA). "Army Hears Richardson Dredging Plea." November 8, 1945, p.1.

*Sausalito News* (CA). "Bechtel Gives Full Report on Marinship's Future." November 1, 1945, p.1.

*Sausalito News* (CA). "Industrial Area Street Map Ok'd." March 3, 1949, p. 8.

*Sausalito News* (CA). "Marinship Complete Wartime Operations: Temporary employment for 600; small plant facilities proposed." November 1, 1945, p.3.

*Sausalito News* (CA). "Sausalitoship Is Named Distributor For Higgins Craft." October 25, 1945, p.1.

Sausalito Schools Foundation. *Sausalito Centennial Cookbook.* Leawood, KS: Circulation Service, 1993.

Sausalito Waterfront Planning Committee. "The Sausalito Waterfront Planning Committee Report." Open-file report, September 1981, p. 52.

Schlesinger, Ellen. "You Call This Living?" *New York Times,* November 6, 1976.

San Francisco Preservation Society. "Brief History of the Historic Preservation Movement in the United States and San Francisco." San Francisco Preservation Bulletin, No. 14, 2003, p. 2)

Scott, Mel. *The Future of San Francisco Bay.* Berkeley, CA: Institute of Governmental Studies, 1963.

Selvin, Joel. *The Musical History Tour: A guide to over 200 of the Bay Area's most memorable music sites.* San Francisco: Chronicle Books, 1996.

Sexton, Richard. *The Cottage Book.* San Francisco, CA: Chronicle Books, 1989, p. 73.

Strahan, Jerry E. *Andrew Jackson Higgins and the Boats That Won World War II.* Baton Rough, LA: Louisiana State University Press, 1994.

Tracy, Jack. *Sausalito: Moments in Time.* Ed. Wayne Bonnett. Salt Lake City: Publishers Press, 1993, 166.

U.S. Department of Veteran Affairs. "History of the G.I. Bill." Working paper, 2006. http://www.75anniversary.va.gov/history/gi_bill.htm

Van Loan, Derek. *Sausalito Waterfront Stories.* San Rafael, CA: Epoch Press, 1992.

Viacom Cablevision. *The Anchor Outs of Richardson Bay.* Marin County, CA: Viacom Cablevision, 1989.

*Waldo Point Garlic Press.* "BCDC Papers." March 1977, Vol. 3 #1.

*Waldo Point Garlic Press.* "Chronology." February 14, 1978, Vol. 4 #1, p.1.

*Waldo Point Garlic Press.* "Kappas' New Harbor: The birds don't care." February 25, 1975.

Walker, Lester. *American Shelter.* Woodstock, NY: The Overlook Press, 1996.

Willoughby, Wes. "Noah Where for Arks to Go." *Sausalito News* (CA), March 10, 1959, p. 13.